ROAD TO REALITY

FINDING MEANING IN A
MEANINGLESS WORLD

Melvin Tinker analyses our modern society with great insight. In this book he provides thoughtful answers to those thinking about the great questions. Unerringly he points the reader to Jesus Christ, the ultimate answer to all the questions.

Rt Revd Frank Retief,
Presiding Bishop of the Church of England in South Africa.

Play a game with this book; stop reading it when you don't read something striking on the next page—I just kept going and going.

Rico Tice
All Souls Church, Langham Place,
Author of Christianity Explored

ROAD TO REALITY

FINDING MEANING IN A MEANINGLESS WORLD
MELVIN TINKER

CHRISTIAN FOCUS

Copyright © Melvin Tinker 2004

ISBN 1-85792-958-6

Published in 2004
by
Christian Focus Publications, Geanies House,
Fearn, Ross-shire, IV20 1TW, Scotland

www.christianfocus.com

Cover design by Alister MacInnes

Printed and bound by
Cox & Wyman, Reading, Berkshire

Contents

For Roy and Judith—
their inspiration and kindness.

Preface

One of my most vivid childhood memories comes from when I was about 5 years old. I was in a busy open market on a day out with my Grandfather, which was always a delight. But that delight soon turned sour as, when we momentarily stopped at a stall to peruse the wares, I let go of my Grandfather's hand and turned only to discover that he had gone. It is not that easy for a small boy to make his way through a large crowd of grown ups. Panic and fear gripped my little heart. All sorts of thoughts ran through my mind. 'Would I ever see my family again?' 'Would I be placed in an orphanage?' The story did end happily. I made my way to a nearby shop, was wonderfully fussed over by the women who worked there, only to be retrieved by my Grandfather and a relieved looking policeman, who saw me through the shop window. If being lost is a terrifying experience, being found is one of the most exhilarating.

However, it is possible to be lost in ways, which though not physical, are just as real. We have all had the experience of following a reasoned argument, or the workings of a mathematical formula, only to exclaim part of the way through: 'Stop, you have lost me.' But more poignant, is the sense of lostness permeating the lives of many people living in the post-modern West. Listen to these words of a fourteen year old: 'Why am I here? What have I done? Why was I born? Who cares about me? I am me. I must suffer because I am me. Why do I live? For love, for happiness? Why should I not commit suicide? I hate this world. I hate my parents and my home—though why, I do not know. I searched for truth but I only found uncertainty. I was thwarted in my search for love. Where can I find happiness? I do not know. Perhaps I shall never know.' Before we dismiss such thoughts as the musings of a disturbed adolescent, the newscaster Anna Ford, now in her mid fifties, said this: 'Life is terribly short and a bit of a joke at our expense. You wonder what it's all about. Getting older has enormous compensations. But I do wonder how I will live. Will I continue working? Will I be lonely when the children leave? I know that if I haven't discovered what I am good at and done it, when I lie on my death bed nothing will compensate for not being fulfilled. I will feel empty.' It appears that the sense that life is some sort of journey is a universal phenomenon, but along with it is the deeper sense of disorientation and lostness. Plutarch wrote: 'The soul is in exile and a wanderer.'

In order to orientate ourselves aright, gain direction and purpose, a map is required. Of course, many today would dismiss the notion of any 'big-picture', which makes sense of life, as being in itself a hopeless wish. But that would be to prejudge the issue. What if our shared instinct is right, that life is a journey with a definite purpose in view—a purpose that comes to us from outside rather than being dreamt up by ourselves? Most of the major world philosophies and religions have claimed this to be the case and have sought to supply such a map.

The Christian faith is no different in this matter. That is the claim made by its founder Jesus Christ and its foundation documents, the Bible. As with any map, the acid test comes in its usefulness as a guide. Does it actually 'fit' with our experience and can it be shared with others? Does the map make sense of itself (with all the different parts hanging together) and with the 'real world', including the experience of previous generations? This does not mean that the ultimate authority is 'experience' in a subjective sense, but rather that what experience intimates, what the Christian message explains, and what the Christian message teaches, experience corroborates.

This book is an attempt to sketch out the Christian 'road map to reality'. It invites the reader to look at the claims of the Bible and how it engages with some of the deep issues of life. It calls the reader to examine his or her own journey so far, and to consider whether a change in direction using another map is called for.

There is no substitute for reading God's road map for yourself—the Bible—to weigh up its trustworthiness (which, may I add, has been well attested to by millions of people from around the world and throughout the ages). But as they say, (to change the picture): 'The proof of the pudding is in the eating'. A map, left on the shelf, gathering dust, is of no functional use. It has to be taken down, opened, and followed. That is the challenge of this little book: Look at Christianity for yourself and to see if it 'rings true.' One thing I can guarantee—you will be surprised.

1

The Animal That Asks:
The Search for Meaning

Pablo Picasso was by all accounts a creative genius. But
many of his friends described him as a monster. Long
before Leonardo de Caprio and Kate Winslet graced the
big screen, Picasso said: 'When I die it will be a shipwreck,
and as when a huge ship sinks, many people all around
will be sucked down with it.' That is exactly what
happened. When he died in 1973 at the grand old age of
ninety-one, three of those closest to him committed
suicide—his second wife Jacqueline, an early mistress
Marie-Therese and his grandson Pablito. Several others
had psychiatric breakdowns, including his first wife Olga
and his most famous mistress, Dora Maar. In the book
Life with Picasso, Francois Gilot recalls the ten years she
had as his third mistress. She points out that for Picasso
there were only two types of women—'godesses and
doormats' and sooner or later everyone went from the
first category to the second. Dora Maar, who preceded

Gilot as Picasso's mistress, once said to him, 'You are the devil', whereupon Picasso branded her with a cigarette held to her cheek, stopping because, as he put it, 'I may still want to look at you.' He once told Gilot, 'Everytime I change wives I should bury the last one. That way I'd be rid of them.' There is no doubt that such behaviour was linked to his atheism. Picasso was an avowed follower of the philosopher Nietzsche and was once heard muttering, 'I am god, I am god.' He acted like it too, driven to produce art and exercise a strangling power over people. If there is no God and so no objective basis for deciding what is right and wrong, good and bad, then why not do what Picasso did? In such a universe, 'might is right'.

But you may respond, 'Get real. Where would we be if everyone acted like that?' That is precisely the challenge the Bible lays down, calling *us* to 'get real', that is, to be intellectually consistent by asking what happens when we try to assess life mainly from an 'experience it and see' approach as many are doing today. How far does it take us? Is it possible to get any satisfactory meaning at all?

One book in the Bible which does this is the book of Ecclesiastes.[1] If ever there was a book for the twenty-first century here it is. The man who is writing this is called, 'Teacher' (1:1) and 'king over Israel' (1:12), who decided to devote his life to studying 'everything under heaven' (1:13). That is one ambitious project! What we have is, in effect, his final dissertation. He begins his thesis by asking a realistic question, which gives rise to a realistic assessment, and ends with a realistic answer.

---

[1] See Appendix for full text. All following numerical references in this chapter refer to Ecclesiastes.

A realistic question

Here is the realistic question: 'What does man gain from all his labours under the sun?'—literally—'What profit is there in life?' (1:3). Or as we might say, 'What is the bottom line?' Is it possible to attain success, meaning, and value in this life, and be satisfied with it? If so, how? If not, then what is the point of living?

This drive for meaning and purpose is a deep-seated one. Back in 1932, in his famous speech entitled 'My Credo', Albert Einstein put it this way: 'Our situation on this earth seems strange. Everyone of us appears here involuntarily and uninvited for a short stay, without knowing the whys and the wherefore.' The actress Jessica Lang felt the same: 'The main thing that I sensed back in my childhood,' she said, 'was this inescapable yearning that I could never satisfy. Even now at times I experience an inescapable loneliness and isolation.' This gut feeling that we are somethings and not nothings, made for Someone or something more, drives us to ask the question: Why?

According to the psychiatrist Viktor Frankle, himself a victim of the Nazi concentration camp, 'The will to find meaning is the primary motivational force in man.' The literary critic George Steiner says simply, 'More than homo sapiens, we are homo quarens, the animal that asks and asks.' We can't help it. Sometimes we try and avoid it, but the question keeps returning to haunt us— maybe in the small hours of the morning, perhaps after a relationship has ended and certainly when faced with death and bereavement, we ask, 'What is it all about?'

A realistic assessment

Our writer goes on to give a realistic assessment. What does life *feel* like, as he puts it, 'under the sun?' His experience is universal, exactly the same as yours and mine—'Meaningless! Meaningless!'—a phrase which appears over and over again and forms the two book ends of this whole essay (1:2; 12:8). What is he saying? That there is no purpose at all? No. The word translated 'meaningless' is *hebel*, which could be rendered 'bubbles'. That is, life as we encounter it seems so fleeting, transitory, a chasing after the wind, it has that 'here today gone tomorrow' quality about it. It is like trying to grab a bubble, no sooner do you have it in your grasp than it pops and is gone. That is what life *feels* like 'under heaven' from a purely experiential point of view. And *whatever* activity we turn to it will *always* feel the same, never totally satisfying.

Eat, drink and be merry

To what do people turn in order to find the 'bottom line of life'? There is pleasure, of course (hedonism): 'I thought in my heart, "Come now, I will test you with pleasure to find out what is good." But that also proved to be meaningless. "Laughter," I said, "is foolish. And what does pleasure accomplish?" I tried cheering myself with wine, and embracing folly—my mind still guiding me with wisdom. I wanted to see what was worth while for men to do under heaven during the few days of their lives' (2:1–3).

Here is part of an article which appeared in a secular counselling magazine: 'He's twenty-nine, he has a good job, his own flat, he is in a stable relationship and he is having a mid-life crisis. "It crept upon me by stealth," says Patrick Winston, a publishing executive from Bath. "I had a great job, a partner, a good social life—everything I'd wanted, but gradually this sense of ennui took over and it left me feeling blank and demotivated. I started to feel that my life—including me—was fraudulent. I kept thinking: what next? I went through a period of heavy promiscuity, which made things worse. I felt that all that was in front of me was the same—acquisition of wealth and status, which had come to mean nothing to me. I became impotent, started drinking heavily and hated myself.'" The article goes on to point out that the mid-life crisis is creeping downward and hitting younger people. As the writer says; 'We are living harder, and burning out sooner. The world is dogged by short-termism, in relationships, in work—and this accelerates the process of disenchantment.' The writer of Ecclesiastes agrees entirely.

Fame—'I want to live for ever'?

What about fame? Is there something in that, given the flourishing 'celeb' culture? Is that the way forward? This man has tried that route too: 'Better a poor but wise youth than an old but foolish king who no longer knows how to take warning. The youth may have come from prison to the kingship, or he may have been born in poverty within his kingdom. I saw that all who lived and walked under the sun followed the youth, the king's successor. There was no end to all the people who were before them. But those who came later were not pleased with the successor. This too is meaningless, a chasing after the wind' (4:13–16). This is a rags to riches story, the climb from prison to palace. But once you reach the top and become *the* celebrity then the only way is down, with all the anxiety that brings, as he says, 'Those who came later *were not* pleased with their successor.' Is that what life is all about? Getting the good qualification so that you can get that good job with the good salary, in order to buy the big house with the big mortgage and big car, and then get the big ulcer?

Let's think about someone else who has reached the top—Madonna. She arrived in New York City with just $35 in her pocket. Within a matter of a few years she was a multimillionaire. Do you know what she says about all of this? She was driven. This is how she describes her experience: 'When my mother died, all of a sudden I was going to be the best student, get the best grades; I was going to become the best singer, the best dancer, the most famous singer in the world. Everybody was going to love me.' Then she adds, 'I am a very tormented person. I want to be happy.'

Education, education, education?

Perhaps education, pursuing knowledge for knowledge's sake, rather than just as a meal ticket, is what we should be living for? The Teacher has explored that blind alley: 'I undertook great projects: I built houses for myself and planted vineyards. I made gardens and parks and planted all kinds of fruit trees in them. I made reservoirs to water groves of flourishing trees' (2:4–6). This fellow was doing a David Attenborough before David Attenborough! He wanted to find out how things tick—he was into science. A good thing, but not a lasting thing. Isn't it strange how quickly those things, which seemed so important at the time, begin to fade. Do you remember all that hard work for those GCSEs or A levels or a degree? Do you remember how you felt once those grades were posted on the school notice board? It was terrific (if you got the grades you wanted). How do you feel about them now? Not that much I would guess. Good things which are not lasting things.

What makes it all worse is that there is so much in this world which is simply unfair. There are bad things which make life hard to take. 'There is something else meaningless on earth: righteous men who get what the wicked deserve, and wicked men who get what the righteous deserve' (8:14). That is pretty obvious. Many a saint has died in agony at the stake and many a tyrant has died peacefully in his sleep. What are we to make of that? Life seems mixed up, a combination of the good, the bad and the ugly.

The good, the bad and the ugly

If there is no God, then all you are left with is the ugly. Good and bad have no meaning. If we are the result of a cosmic accident, then, by definition, accidents do not have a purpose. Can you honestly look at yourself in the mirror and say truthfully, 'I am an accident. I am of no more significance than spilt milk?' National newspapers have highlighted the rising incidence of suicide amongst young people and especially young men. It is one of the most pressing concerns of our society. While there are no doubt several factors at work—unstable family life, pressure for success—there is one deep and underlying cause, a lack of identity and significance. We are no longer sure who we are. If we see ourselves as nothings (which is the logic of living in an impersonal universe), it is not long before we start treating ourselves, and others, as nothings.

A realistic response

What is the explanation? Why do we live in a world which is made up of the good, the bad and the ugly? This brings us to the realistic answer which is embedded throughout the essay, for example: 'I have seen the burden God has laid on men. He has made everything beautiful in its time. He has also set eternity in the hearts of men; yet they cannot fathom what God has done from beginning to end. I know that there is nothing better for men than to be happy and do good while they live. That everyone may eat and drink, and find satisfaction in all his toil—this is the gift of God. I know that everything God does will endure forever; nothing can be added to it and nothing taken from it. God does it so that men will revere him' (3:10–14). Here is an account of reality which puts the pieces together in the jigsaw and makes sense—the biblical picture. Here is a map we can follow with confidence.

There is a sense in which we *are* to find satisfaction in the things mentioned. It is great to have fun, it is good to learn, it is right that we use our abilities and make something of our work and station in life. But what these things *cannot* do is to bear the weight we often place upon them to provide deep, *lasting* meaning. They were never meant to perform that function. That would be like placing an articulated lorry on a frail wooden bridge, it will collapse. Similarly, our lives collapse too when we try to invest these good things with too much value because they then become idolatrous. Instead of us seeing them as gifts which are meant to lead us on to the Giver, we become besotted with the gifts and treat them as gods and they eventually destroy us, as being consumed with money, sex and power are destroying people's lives today.

But the Bible confirms and corrects our experience by revealing to us the true God, and telling us why the world is as it is and why we feel as we feel.

So what is this God like?

First, he is an *all-wise God*, he has made everything beautiful in its time—just right. That is why we live in a 'universe' not a 'multiverse', a cosmos rather than a chaos. Atheism doesn't explain that.

Secondly, he is an *all-personal God*, for as the Teacher says, he has put eternity in the hearts of men and women. There is that intuitive knowledge that we are made for a love relationship with our Maker which is meant to take us into eternity. We are not just animals, but animals that ask, 'Why?' God tells us why; he has made us in his image so that we can only find our true selves when we are properly related to him.

In the third place, he is the *all-giving God,* giving us wine, food, and friendships which we are meant to enjoy, and in turn be thankful to him. This sense of gratitude we feel when we have passed an exam, or when a baby is born, is not a *proof* that God exists but a *pointer*. As Dante Gabriel Rosseti said: 'The worst moment for an atheist is when he is genuinely thankful but has nobody to thank.' Or as G. K. Chesterton put it, 'If my children wake up on Christmas morning and have someone to thank for putting candy in their stocking, have I no one to thank for putting two feet in mine?' We have all felt like that at sometime in our lives. It is not incidental, we are meant to pick up the signal and follow it to its source.

But what about the bad things or the things that puzzle us? Where does belief in God fit into that?

First of all, it is obvious that if we live in a marvellous and complex universe and we are small finite creatures, then some things are always going to baffle us. We can't bring God down to our size, otherwise he wouldn't be God: 'Consider what God has done: Who can straighten what he has made crooked? When times are good, be happy; but when times are bad, consider: God has made the one as well as the other' (7:13–14). In the second place, the Bible is clear that a lot of the problems we face are of our own doing, not God's. We have already seen that the Teacher talks about 'evil men' and wickedness. The Bible is realistic about those things too. If there is no God, then as the Oxford scientist Richard Dawkins says, evil is just another way of describing how we dance to our own DNA. But we know differently, evil is when we snub our Maker and like Picasso start acting like God. We all do it. When we have a world populated with billions of people acting in this way then what else are we going to get but cheating, lying, stealing, wars and the like?

What we need to do is to pick up the strands given to us and follow them in order to find out about this God who made us, loves us and cares for us in a world we have messed up. But how? Do we have to be like this man, the Teacher, and go on a long search? Not really. The second half of God's road map to reality, the New Testament, introduces us to someone else who was also called 'The Teacher'. He too is described as King of Israel, one whose wisdom is greater than even that of King Solomon. He speaks of himself as a seeker. Not someone seeking the truth, indeed he says of himself, 'I am the Truth'. Rather, he is a seeker of people—people like you and me. In Luke 19:10 he says, 'The Son of Man came to *seek* and to *save* that which was lost.' To all those who want true life, quality life, he says, 'I am the Life.' To those who want to make sense of this broken world and do something about it, he says, 'I am the Truth.' To those who desperately want to follow the gifts to the end to which they point—God—he says, 'I am the Way…if you have seen me, you have seen the Father.' And that someone is the Lord Jesus Christ, the God who became man. He came in order to die impaled on a cross, giving himself as a sacrifice for all our wrongdoing, taking the punishment in our place that is rightly ours for the appalling way we have treated our Maker. Then, by rising from the dead as the eternal ruler, he ensures that death does not make a final mockery of our accomplishments. He gives value and dignity to our lives as we come to know him personally now and will know him fully then in heaven.

The question is: Do you know God personally and are you loving and joyfully serving him? Do you know the Giver and not just the gifts? Here in the Bible is the map to follow in order to find him. As it says at the end of this book: 'Now all has been heard; here is the conclusion of the matter: Fear God and keep his commandments, for this is the whole duty of man' (12:13).

2

Where Do I Come From?
The Search for Origins

Several years ago the famous economist E. F. Schumacher, author of the book, *Small is Beautiful*, gave a talk in London which began with an account of his recent trip to St. Petersburg, Russia, which then went under the communist name of Leningrad. Despite having a map in hand which he followed painstakingly, he realised that he was lost. What he saw on the paper didn't fit with what he saw right in front of his eyes, namely, several huge Russian Orthodox churches. They weren't on the map and yet he was certain he knew which street he was on. 'Ah,' said an Intertourist guide, trying to be helpful, 'that's simple. We don't show churches on our maps.'

Schumacher then went on to say: 'It then occurred to me that this is not the first time I had been given a map which failed to show things I could see right in front of my eyes. All through school and university I had been given maps of life and knowledge on which there was hardly a trace of many of the things that I most cared about and that seemed to me to be of the greatest possible importance to the conduct of my life.' In other words, what he had been taught, and picked up from the media, missed out issues of faith which were so vital to him.

Map makers

The fact is we all have 'mental maps' with which we operate, some are thought out, others are simply picked up and assimilated without much reflection at all. What these maps are meant to do is to help us understand how the world works and how we fit into it. Sometimes these maps are called 'world views' which, as the term suggests, is how we view the world. And this is not merely the stuff of academics. Everybody has a world view. We all assume certain things to be true—maybe about the value of human life or its lack of value, what the purpose of life is, and so on. What is more, the view we hold will affect the way we live. For example, many non-Christian western intellectuals of the nineteenth century were simply racist. Some used Darwin's theory of evolution in order to try to demonstrate that some races were superior to others and it was a 'given' that this was so. One such man was Herbert Spencer who popularised Darwin's theory and argued that different races were going through different stages of 'cultural evolution' which had to be taken into account when assessing the level of understanding of different people groups. So, he said, Australians had no power of concentration or integrated ideas, and American Negro children educated alongside whites did not 'correspondingly advance in their learning' (i.e. they could go only so far and no further). Of course this influenced social and educational policy. These people were not stupid, they honestly believed they were right and had the backing of science to boot! The point is that we all have a way of viewing what we think is reality, and some of those maps are desperately flawed and have drastic effects—some leading to the gas chambers of Auschwitz. Therefore, we need to make sure that we have got a good map; for how you treat your girlfriend, raise your children, or whether you cheat in exams or not, will all depend upon your world view.

But how do you know that the way you are thinking about life is one which corresponds to the way things are?

Any world view has to satisfactorily answer four big questions: 1. Where do I come from?—the question of origins. 2. Who am I?—the question of significance. 3. Why is the world in such a mess?—the question of evil. 4. Is there a future?—the question of purpose. It is no good having a world view or faith, if you will, which misses out on any of these questions and ignores the hard edges of reality. Our map must have a good 'fit' with our experience of the world.

Let us consider the first question: Where do we come from? There is a story of a little boy who came home from school one day and said to his father: 'Dad, where do I come from?' This was the moment the father had been dreading. So he took a deep breath, sat down and painfully worked his way through the facts of life. The boy sat there, wide eyes, hardly believing what he was hearing. Then when the father had finished, relieved that the ordeal was over, he said, 'Well, son, are there any questions?' The boy replied, 'No Dad, it's just that Johnny next door said he comes from Birmingham and I wondered where I came from?'

The question of origins is such an important one because it is on this that all the other answers about who we are, the problem of evil and the purpose of life, turn.

WYSIWYG

Let's take the world view which the majority of people in the West hold today and which is taken on board almost without question. It is the world view called secular materialism or 'What You See Is What You Get'—WYSIWYG. At its most basic level it is the view that we are all the result of a great cosmic accident. There may have been a 'Big Bang', it will all end in the 'Big Crunch', and we find ourselves here thrown up as accidents by pure materialistic forces. There is no God, no spiritual realm, and so we have to make the best of a bad job.

The American astronomer Carl Sagan popularised this on TV several years ago in the series Cosmos. He said, 'The cosmos is all there is and ever will be.' He argued that all life was simply a product of nature, and therefore we are on the same level as all other animals in terms of value and significance. Sagan tried to follow this through and espouse animal rights, until one day, he was diagnosed with a potentially fatal blood disease. He was told that there was no cure for it, except one possible bone marrow transplant. But the doctor warned him, 'Dr Sagan, we know exactly what you have believed all your life about medical research on animals, and we want you to know that this treatment has been developed by research on animals.' A tough moral dilemma. How long do you think it took Sagan to make his decision? Around twenty seconds! You can't live with that world view; the map is faulty. It doesn't make sense, explain why we *feel* important, why we believe in right and wrong, or why we intuitively feel that there is life after death. The map is hopeless because it doesn't deal with life as we know it.

While I was in Australia I was given the use of a car with a satellite navigation system. This computer, which was linked to a satellite, meant that you could enter your destination and a map would appear while a voice gave you directions: 'Turn right at the next junction'. It was great, except that my friend who owned the car once had to go into a newly constructed tunnel, which went right under a major river. The system didn't know about this tunnel and it threw a fit as it appeared he had drowned head first! What is the point of a map, however sophisticated, with satellite link up, if it misses out something as vital as a tunnel! Sadly, the life maps many people are operating with are about as useful as that. They are of no comfort when, for example, a crisis hits.

Supposing you have a little boy and he is terminally ill–is that it? Is his death of no more significance than the death of a rat? It comes down to that if you believe in secular materialism. But instinctively we react against such an idea, might this not suggest that we need a new map?

The perfect fit

Let's look at the only viable alternative, a map that has all the main features on it and fits perfectly. Let us go back and consider the first few verses in Genesis.

At the outset, let me clear away a common misunderstanding, namely, the alleged conflict between the Genesis account of creation and the findings of modern science. I would want to suggest that Genesis and science are dealing with two different types of question. Science attempts to answer the 'how' question, by what processes does the natural world operate? Accordingly, there are scientific descriptions of reality in terms of physical laws, biological models and so on. But what the Bible is mainly concerned with is the more profound and important 'why' questions: What is the purpose of this world? What is its meaning? We might even say that it focuses on the 'who' question—who is the person behind the whole show? Science cannot answer those questions for it is solely concerned with mechanism not meaning. Let me use a simple illustration. A scientist can come along and analyse the text of this book. As a *scientist* he could give a full and sufficient description of it in terms of the chemical components of the ink, the cellulose content of the paper etc. In its own terms, it could be totally complete. But what the scientist could not give purely *as a scientist,* is the meaning of the book. That is a literary question, not a scientific one. What would also be certain is that his account wouldn't include me as the author of the book. The 'who' and the 'why' lie beyond scientific terms of reference. Likewise, in principle, there is no contradiction between the Bible's accounts of the origin of the universe and that of modern science. Even *if* one could produce a complete account of the origin of the world in terms of the big bang, an expanding universe, biological evolution and the like, that still does not rule out the Genesis account which is complementary. It uses evocative imagery which is applicable to every culture at every time to describe the fact that whatever *processes* God may have used to bring about this world and keep it going (and those questions of process need to be decided on scientific grounds), he is the one behind it all and working through it all. God is the one who gives it meaning and purpose. In short, rather than seeing the Bible and science as being *contradictory*, they can be thought of as *complementary*. All of this we see in those first three verses.

Verse 1: 'In the beginning *God created* the heavens and the earth.' Our meaningfulness and the meaningfulness of the universe stems from the fact that we are *created* by a personal God, for only created things can have meaning. Imagine that before you is a microphone. What meaning does it have? In and of itself it has no meaning. The meaning it has is what its creator, owner and judge gives it. Whoever made it, did so with a purpose in mind, so that it can pick up a voice or sound and then once fed into an amplifier and speaker project that sound. The creator gave it that meaning. But once it has been sold the *owner* can give it meaning. If you were the owner you *could* take it and stir tea with it or use it as truncheon or scratch your back with it. Those may be odd uses, but meaningful uses nonetheless. But one day its judge will give it meaning too, and evaluate, it saying, 'This is a useless microphone, it no longer works, I am going to throw it in the bin.' The Maker of it, the Owner of it and the Judge of it—all give it meaning. That is exactly what the Bible says is the case of this universe and our place in it. The microphone is made to do the job it was designed to do. I am no expert but I would imagine it is possible to find one process to make microphones in one way and a different process to make microphones in another way. From one point of view, the process used doesn't matter too much provided that the end result is exactly what the maker, owner and judge intend. So it is with us. We have a Maker, Owner and Judge, who are one and the same—God—and who has used natural processes to bring us about. We live in an incredibly complex and ordered universe. It is vast, beautiful and breathtaking. It is a remarkable universe in so many ways. One of the things scientists are now telling us is that it appears to be the only kind of universe which has all the right conditions, all coming together at the right time, in the right sort of way, to produce you and me. It is called the *anthropic principle* and non-Christian scientists like Professor Paul Davies are championing it. Even following the big bang hypothesis the physical constraints of this universe are so finely tuned that it would only take a fraction of a fraction of a fraction difference in anything at that beginning and there would be nothing. This is what Davies writes: 'The very fact that the universe is creative and that laws have permitted complex structures to emerge and develop to the point of self-consciousness…is for me powerful evidence that there is "something going on" behind it all. The impression of design is overwhelming.' That is exactly what Genesis 1:1 is saying. There is a Someone going on behind it all, and in it all, and that Someone is the all-knowing, all-powerful, personal God.[1]

But how does this personal God relate to the world he has made, owns and judges? We are told: 'Now the earth was formless and empty, darkness was over the surface of the deep, and the Spirit of God was hovering over the waters. And God said…' (1:2-3a). The rest of the chapter is a moving account of the way in which

[1] See Appendix for text of Genesis 1. All following numerical references in this chapter refer to Genesis.

form is given to that which was formless and content given to that which was empty. How does God relate to the world and bring about his purposes in that world? By his Spirit and his Word: the 'Spirit' was hovering over the deep like a bird, and straight away 'God *said* let there be … and there was …' (1:3). The Hebrew word, *ruach,* translated Spirit, could also be rendered 'wind' or 'breath'. This tells us something important about the relationship between God, his Spirit, his Word and his creation.

Word and Spirit

First of all, God's Spirit and God's Word always go together. Just as my words are carried out on my breath, so it is with God's Word, carried out on the breath of His Spirit. As God's Word is taught, faithfully and truly, then his Spirit is at work.

Several years ago there was a saying doing the rounds in Christian circles: 'All Spirit no Word we blow up. All Word no Spirit we dry up. But Word and Spirit together we grow up.' It may be a neat saying, but it borders on the blasphemous. Do we believe that the Spirit of God through which God brings about a creation as wonderful as ours can 'blow up' people? Do we believe that the sweet Word of God which brings life into people and nourishes them, 'dries up' people? In the Bible, whenever God's Spirit is at work it is through his Word, and as the Word is at work it is in the power of the Holy Spirit.

At the beginning of time God related to the universe by his Spirit and by his Word and he still does the same today. You do not find God in a subjective mystical experience, produced by chanting, or fasting or singing songs around a candle. He is encountered through his

Word. That is why we must get stuck into the Bible—if we don't, we won't be relating to God.

The wonderful thing is that when we turn to the New Testament we are enabled to see more clearly just who, rather than what, the Spirit and Word are which were bringing the universe into being. John's Gospel opens with the line: 'In the beginning was the Word, and the Word was with God, and the Word was God. He was with God in the beginning. Through him all things were made.' This Word is *a person*, also God. Later in the chapter we are told that this Word is God the Son who came to this earth 2000 years ago as the person of Jesus of Nazareth (John 1:14). The Maker became a man so that God could relate to men. He related to the world through his 'Word', the word incarnate—Jesus. What is more, we are told later in the same Gospel that Jesus would send another one like himself, another person, called the Holy Spirit, also God, who is the Spirit of Truth (John 14:16). He would enable the apostles to remember Jesus' teaching, and what they have remembered has been written down for us under the inspiration of the Spirit in what is often called the Word of God, the Bible (John 14:26). We are also told that in order to have a personal relationship with God we have to be born again by the Spirit as we trust in Jesus, so that becoming Christian is like being a new creation (John 3:3). Just as in the beginning the Spirit of God moved over dark, deep waters and when God spoke his Word he brought light and life, so now God's Spirit moves in dark spiritually dead human hearts, and when the Word of the Gospel is explained, he brings inner light and life. This is the way the apostle Paul puts it: 'For God, who said, "Let light shine out of darkness," made his light shine in our hearts to give us the light of the knowledge of the glory of God in the face of Christ' (2 Cor. 4:6).

What this comes down to is that we were made *by* a personal God, Father, Son and Holy Spirit and were made *for* this personal God. We can only know the Father by believing in God the Son, enabled by God the Spirit. This entire universe belongs to him and so do our lives.

Which map are you actually following? If you are simply living mainly for yourself, what you can get out of life, moving on from one thrill to the next, besotted with money and possessions, what you are going to eat and wear, then no matter how religious you may think you are, or how ever much you may want to *call* yourself a Christian, you are following the wrong map. You are acting as if there is no God who made you and to whom one day you are going to give an account. To be frank, that needs to be put right. The God who made you has also come to rescue you so that he can put you back in touch with himself. This 'Word', the 'God said' of Genesis 1, became the man Jesus in order to die on a cross and to rise again from the dead. He sends his life-giving Holy Spirit into our lives so that we can know him, have meaning and true life. This is a life which is given over in the sacrificial service of others.

Where do I come from? The answer is: God. There is no greater need in our lives than to know him who made us and obediently serve him who loves us.

3

Who Am I?
The Search for Identity

The journalist Bernard Levin wrote these words: 'To put it bluntly, have I time to discover why I was born before I die? I have not managed to answer that question yet, and however many years I have before me they are certainly not as many as there are behind. There is an obvious danger in leaving it too late. Why do I have to know why I was born? Because, I am unable to believe it was an accident, and if it wasn't one, it must have meaning.'

A new Herod?
But of course there are many people who do believe that life is simply an accident and attempt to apply that belief to the moral complexities of living. One such man is Dr Peter Singer who teaches ethics at Princeton University and is one of the world's most influential ethicists. In his book, *Practical Ethics*, he takes as his starting point what he calls, 'the principle of equal consideration of interests'. That is the view that the interests of all human beings

must be taken into account when assessing the consequences of an action. This principle, he argues, extends to other self-conscious beings who can suffer, and only such beings can be said to have 'interests'. He puts forward the idea that human beings can be thought of in two ways—as belonging to the species *Homo sapiens*, or being a person. He defines a person as a 'self-conscious or rational being' who can therefore make decisions. He wants to maintain that some primates—monkeys and apes—are also self-conscious to some extent and so could be described as persons. Therefore, being a member of the species *Homo sapiens* is not a sufficient reason for being thought of as a person. This has very far-reaching implications. It means that adult primates are persons, but a newborn infant is not. It is therefore not intrinsically wrong to kill a newborn baby who is not self-conscious, whereas it would be wrong to kill an ape who is supposed to be self-conscious. Singer does not suggest that newborn children should be killed if they are healthy and wanted, but that they *could* be if they were unhealthy and unwanted. He says that strict conditions should be placed on permissible infanticide, but that 'these restrictions might owe more to the effects of infanticide on others than to the intrinsic wrongness of killing an infant.' Here, then, is the new King Herod.

This man is serious. As the debate about euthanasia raises its head once more, this sort of view is going to be increasingly held. After all, it is consistent with the world view called secular materialism or WYSIWYG—'What You See Is What You Get'—there is no God and so no ultimate source of value.

Paganism reinvented

When you think about it, this new view is really an old view. It is the old view of paganism. Infanticide was certainly taught by the Greeks like Plato. What, therefore, happened between the old paganism, in which the ill and deformed could be left to die exposed on a hilltop, and the new paganism which in some cases allows newborns to die deprived of water and nutrients in a hospital ward? What gave rise to the view that human beings were unique, had dignity and therefore were to be cared for, that there was such a thing as the *sanctity* of life? There was, of course, the rise of Christianity. This is what Singer, who is an atheist, has to say, 'If we go back to the origins of Western civilisation, to Greek or Roman times, we find that membership of Homo sapiens was not sufficient to guarantee that one's life would be protected. Greeks and Romans killed deformed or weak infants by exposing them to the elements on a hilltop. Plato and Aristotle thought that the state should enforce the killing of deformed infants. The change in Western attitudes to infanticide since Roman times is, like the doctrine of the sanctity of human life of which it is a part, a product of Christianity. Perhaps it is now possible to think about these issues without assuming the Christian moral framework that has, for so long, prevented any fundamental reassessment.' In other words, with Christianity out of the way as a serious intellectual option, let us think the unthinkable.

This world view of Singer's may sound radical, but is it realistic? While any belief, however harebrained, can be taught, not every belief can be lived. And that goes for Singer's because he pays large sums of money to support his mother who has Alzheimer's disease. He justifies this by saying that it provides work for a lot of people and so does some good. He can't live with his philosophy. Something deep inside which makes him act as if his mother *is* valuable, even though, sadly, she is less responsive than some other primates Singer thinks should have rights. Why is that? Why does his heart contradict his head? The Bible tells us why—we are created significant by an all-knowing, all-personal God.

What's the difference?

What is it that makes you and me different to an ape? Genetically there is little difference. Humans and apes share 98.5% of the same genetic material. But it is that 1.5% difference which makes all the difference in the world—for what results is a creature unlike any other.

This is the way the book of Genesis puts it: 'Then God said, "Let us make man in our image, in our likeness, and let them rule over the fish of the sea and the birds of the air, over the livestock, over all the earth, and over all the creatures that move along the ground." So God created man in his own image, in the image of God he created him; male and female he created them' (1:26–7).[1] What is the difference between us and the rest of the animal kingdom? It is that in some way we are 'God-like'—made in the image of God. Interestingly enough, nowhere in the Bible is this ever defined. Since God is Spirit, it can't mean that we are *physically* like him, so we must get rid of those Michaelangelo ideas of God being an old man with a white beard. What it means to be made in the image of God is given to us in this passage. It operates at both the level of *doing* and *being*. What are humans meant

[1] See Appendix for text of Genesis 1. All following numerical references in this chapter refer to Genesis.

to *do* under God? The answer is that they are meant to *rule* 'over the fish of the sea, birds of the air' and so on. That is, they are to reflect in some measure what *God* does as the loving ruler of the universe, they are to creatively care for that which he has made and owns and so they are ultimately accountable to him. But this image also shows itself in the way we are made to *relate* to one another: 'in the image of God he created him—*male and female* he created them.' Just as in some way God within his own being is a community of love as Father, Son and Holy Spirit—'let *us* make man in *our* image' (1:26)—the way we relate to each other, especially in marriage, should reflect that. In other words, our true significance and worth are to be found when we act as God means us to act and relate as he intends us to relate.

Right relationships

Let's take the matter of *relationships* first.

You may have seen the film *Cast Away* starring Tom Hanks. It is about a businessman who finds himself stranded on a desert island. It is a film which is enough to put you off flying and dentistry for life! This is no Robinson Crusoe idyll. It is harsh, dangerous and desperate. There is no human or even animal contact to be made. So what does he do? He imprints a face on a volleyball which happened to be in a parcel carried by the crashed plane and calls it 'Wilson'. For four years 'Wilson' is the only company he has. He talks to him, he devises plans with him and even gets angry with him. This doesn't mean that he has 'lost it', on the contrary, having an imaginary friend in the form of a face on a volleyball keeps the character sane. The point is that we are only truly human in relationships with other humans, so much so, that in extreme circumstances we devise a substitute like Wilson. When does that tiny little baby first feel that he or she matters? Surely it is when they look up and see the sweet smiling face of the mother and all the love it radiates. It is when he or she is lovingly held, fed and cared for, then they know they are of value.

It is not good for man to be alone, says the Bible, for we are made for community. Consider that beautiful account in Genesis 2:18: 'The LORD God said, "It is not good for the man to be alone. I will make a helper suitable for him." And so God brings to Adam a whole variety of animals which were not suitable, for they were *so* unlike man. He needed someone like him, yet different to him, someone who would complement him, a 'better half'—someone with whom he would feel whole, a relationship which would complete the circle of significance. Therefore, we read: 'So the LORD God caused the man to fall into a deep sleep; and while he was sleeping, he took one of the man's ribs and closed up the place with flesh. Then the LORD God made a woman from the rib he had taken out of the man, and he brought her to the man [like a Father presenting the bride to the groom]. The man said "This is now bone of my bones and flesh of my flesh; she shall be called 'woman' for she was taken out of man." For this reason a man will leave his father and mother and be united to his wife, and they will become one flesh' (Gen. 2:21–4).

It is supremely in the marriage relationship that we see a reflection of this image of God. The loving protective care the husband is meant to show to his wife, and the loving obedient support the wife shows to her husband, mirrors something of the relationship between Father, Son, and Holy Spirit. God the Father at the baptism of

Jesus affirms him and sends the Holy Spirit in the form of a dove to strengthen and enable him, while the Son says in Gethsemane, 'Not my will but yours' and obediently goes to the cross to save the world.

It is therefore in the community of the family and the wider community of society, and especially the new community of the church, we are meant to display our God-like image. The image of God is not so much something *within* us, but something expressed *between* us. So when we see a helpless, but terminally ill newborn infant, what is the God-like thing to do? Isn't it to show some care and affection for that baby during its last few hours, as God the giver of life shows care and affection to us, rather than quickly disposing of it as a worthless commodity? What about our business dealings with each other? Following the collapse of Enron, there resulted a serious crisis of confidence on Wall Street. Why? Because people felt no one can be trusted, for people were willing to lie and cheat to make a quick buck. But if this life is all there is, and we are a collection of meaningless atoms, then why not? But if we are made in God's image, then we are being most true to our nature when we are honest and faithful with each other as God is with us.

If we cheat on our wife or boyfriend, or lie to get our way, then not only are we eroding the significance and dignity of the other person, we are demeaning ourselves as we become less and less human. If children bad-mouth their parents and treat them like dirt whose opinions don't matter, and if parents ride rough shod over their children and do not treat them with the respect they deserve, then they too are being sub-human. For God the Son loves his Father and seeks to bring honour to him, and God the Father desires the highest for his Son and those, like you and me, his Son came to save. This raises the question: how God-like are we being in our relationships?

In Colossians 3:9–10 we see the reason Paul gives for the way Christians should and should not be relating: 'Do not lie to each other since you have taken off your old self with its practices and have put on the new self, *which is being renewed in knowledge in the image of its Creator.*' He then goes on to describe how that new self is expressed in how we relate: 'compassion, kindness, humility, gentleness, patience' (3:12). When you are being patient or compassionate with someone, you are being God-like. To be like God is not an ego trip involving power grabbing—that is devilish, it is being self-sacrificing and kind, for that is what God is like.

Right rule

What, then, of that image being shown in how we *rule*? 'The LORD God took the man and put him in the Garden of Eden *to work it and take care of it.* And the LORD God commanded the man, "You are *free* to eat from any tree in the garden, but you must not eat the tree of the knowledge of good and evil, for when you eat of it you will surely die" (2:15–17). Already in chapter 1:28, mankind has received God's blessing with the God-given purpose of 'subduing the earth.' That is, while the world has been created by God and designated 'good'—right for the purposes he intends—human beings are to be, as it were, God's fellow workers in taming that world, harnessing its resources in a responsible way for other people's benefit and God's glory. This picture is developed in Genesis 2 with the man being placed in a park, which kings of the ancient Near East invariably had, and as a priestly monarch he is meant to 'care' for it and work it.

This caring and working is also an expression of his God-like image. That is why work is a good thing and why we should find value and significance in what we do, whether it is paid employment or unpaid—there is dignity in both of these things. But, conversely, when that creativity is taken away from us, that is when we feel so devalued, which is why unemployment is such a devastating thing. Creative work is essential to our nature as human beings.

During the Second World War a commandant of a German concentration camp hit upon a sadistic idea. He took a group of inmates, gave them shovels and sacks and made them shift a pile of sand from one spot to another. When they had done that, they had to put it back again. This went on, day after day, week after week, month after month. Most went mad as a result, some choosing to throw themselves onto the barbed wire and be killed rather than go on. Why? It wasn't because the work was harder than what others in the camp had to do. It was because it was meaningless, having no purpose. As such it smashed the God-given image we all have.

All of these things we see perfectly expressed in Jesus who is *the* 'image of the invisible God' (Col. 1:15). How is this so? First, it is shown by how the Son relates to the Father in humble obedience and service: 'The Son can do nothing by himself; he can do only what he sees his Father doing' (John 5:19). He is not going to 'do his own thing', he loves his Father and knows his ways are good, true and for our best, so he delights in doing them. Reading and obeying the Bible is not drudgery; it is a delight. Secondly, Jesus relates to others in serving through his teaching and healing, and supremely his death. 'I am among you as one who serves', he says. The image of God in Christ is also expressed through how he relates to

43

creation as its ruler—hence the stilling of the storm. What Adam, God's son, was meant to do—relate properly to God, the world and other people—Jesus the second Adam, the Son of God, does perfectly.

It may be that you have been wrestling with this question, 'Who am I?' Perhaps you have been badly let down and hurt, maybe by your parents, perhaps by your husband or wife, or even by the church. For some reason you feel a self-loathing, desperate to receive approval and worth. You want to feel fulfilled, but you feel so empty. If that is you in some measure (and if we are honest it is true of us all to some degree) then here is some very good news indeed. In God's sight you form the pinnacle of his creation and are precious. He invests you with a value that even the angels do not share, for you, unlike them, are made in his image. Certainly that image has been marred by sin, that is why you feel as you do and why people have behaved as they have. But what God has done in his Son is to provide a way whereby that image can slowly be pieced back together. But before we can start relating properly to each other and with our inner selves, we have got to get the most important relationship put right: our relationship with our Maker. We can't reach up to him, but he reaches down to us through his Son, Jesus. He died on a cross so that you could be forgiven, with the self-centredness which cuts us off from him being washed away. He is alive so that as His Holy Spirit comes into your life, he gives you a fresh start so that you can know God as Father. He also puts you into a new family, the church, so that you can begin to live out your God-likeness in giving and receiving God's love with others who also know him as Father. Is that what you have? Is that what you want? Read on, follow the map.

4

The Lost World:
The Search for Order

Have you heard of the difference between an optimist
and a pessimist? The optimist is the person who believes
that this is the best of all possible worlds. The pessimist
is the one who sadly believes he is right! Our world has
not been short of its optimists. In 1516 Thomas More,
of 'A Man for All Seasons' fame, wrote a book called
Utopia, which could be translated 'good place' or 'dream
place'. It depicted an island with fifty-four well-designed
towns, each with 6,000 communities, Spartan in their
values and war hating in their attitudes. There were
gardens for every house, and even euthanasia for the old
and decrepit. More recently, Ian M. Banks has written a
novel, 'Look Windward', in which he sees his Utopia as
existing on another planet which offers its 15 billion
inhabitants every climate, terrain and distraction they
could wish for. Here you can travel a river longer than a
thousand Amazons, or go rafting on molten lava.

But the ideals of Utopia are not restricted to works of fiction. Here is part of the second Humanist Manifesto: 'By using technology wisely, we can control our environment, conquer poverty, modify human behaviour, alter the course of human evolution and cultural development and provide humankind with an unparalleled opportunity for achieving an abundant and meaningful life.' But when attempts are made to translate this into practice, Utopia soon degenerates into Dystopia: a place of torment. This is the stuff of the five-year plans of Stalin in Russia, the Cultural revolution of Mao in China, and the madness of Pol Pot in Cambodia. In seeking to put in place a so-called equal society, social experiments were undertaken which left millions dead and dying through starvation and outright murder. George Orwell saw this clearly in his 1945 satire on the Stalinist state, *Animal Farm*, where it was wryly observed that though all the animals were equal, 'some were more equal than others.'

But we in the West are not in a position to feel morally superior. After the collapse of communism in Eastern Europe and the unprecedented alliance against Iraq at the beginning of the 90s it was the then President George Bush who pronounced a 'new world order'. Such a pronouncement now seems rather hollow. A new world *dis*order more like. The great social experiment of moral liberalisation which began in Britain in the 1960s has conspired to produce the broken families, the drug abuse and the violence we are now experiencing in the twenty-first century. Have you ever wondered why? Why for all the ideals, hopes and aspirations, and the rhetoric of our politicians, left and right, Utopia never arrives? Why it is that our world seems to be a lost world? One of the earliest

Christian thinkers, the apostle Paul, tells us why in Romans chapter 1.[1] It is because, he insists, God is angry: 'The wrath of God is *being* revealed [present tense] from heaven against all the godlessness and wickedness of men who suppress the truth by their wickedness' (1:18).

All this talk of an angry God may come as a shock to some of us: after all, doesn't the Bible tell us that God is love, so how can he be angry with that which he has made? Three things need to be said in response.

All you need is love?

First, God's love and God's anger are not to be thought of as expressions of his nature in exactly the same way. That is, God from all eternity has been love, God *is* love. There has always been that dynamic of giving and receiving within the Godhead, even before the universe was created—the Father eternally loving the Son, the Son eternally loving the Father, embracing each other by the eternal love of the Holy Spirit. But for God to express his anger, something or someone outside of God has to do something to provoke it, namely sin. Sin is a religious word which means that we put ourselves at the centre of the universe instead of God. Therefore, no sin, no anger.

Secondly, God's anger is not like ours. We get angry because we feel hard done by. The girlfriend ignores us; we get angry. We are passed over for promotion; we get angry. Our tutor gives us a low mark; we are angry. Often our anger is disproportionate. It is not so much an eye for an eye, we want two eyes if the truth be known! Our anger can be fitful and selfish; God's anger is measured, often greatly restrained, and concerned with justice.

[1] See Appendix for text of Romans 1. All following numerical references in this chapter refer to Romans.

But in the third place, God's anger and his love are not opposites, he is angry *because* he loves. The opposite of anger is not love, it is indifference.

Imagine that there is a father or mother with a son or daughter. The child falls into a life of stealing and lying, with lazy and destructive habits. Which is the parent who loves them? Is it the one who, with a shrug of the shoulders says, 'Oh it doesn't really matter, it's their life, who am I to interfere?' The result is that they go from bad to worse. Or is it the parent who, angry with what their child is doing to themselves and others, does everything to direct the child to a better way of life, using sanctions and punishment when reason seems to fail? Who would you rather have as your parent? God is like a caring parent. Call it righteous anger if you like: a divine disgust at what evil does to his children, and what evil his children do to each other. Could you honestly believe in a God who smiles as benignly on Adolf Hitler and Dr Barnardo with equal affection? Of course not. As someone once said: The real question is not 'How dare a loving God be angry?' but rather, 'How can a loving God feel anything less?'

The root problem

The real problem with our lost world is not lack of education or the need for more technology or better housing, important though these things may be. The real problem is that we are on the wrong side of God and God is making no secret of the fact. The evidence of his divine disapproval is all around. Notice the two things which provoke it: 'godlessness and wickedness' (1:18). *Godlessness* is our failure as *religious* beings and *wickedness*: our failure as *moral* beings. Those two words are a perfect summary of what the Bible means when it talks about the sinfulness of the human race. We are made in God's image but we reject the norms of spirituality and morality which that image demands. Like Frank Sinatra we have decided to do things our way, not God's way, and we have made a mess. Paul's argument is that we have no excuse for that. There is no excuse for our godlessness for we know enough about God to worship him (1:19), and there is no excuse for our immorality because we know enough about his moral standards to obey him (1:32).

Many people think that God, if he or it exists at all, is an irrelevance. They know nothing about him, so how dare he judge them, anymore than if you do not know that the speed limit is thirty miles an hour, how can you be prosecuted if you exceed it? So, plead ignorance.

The road map of the Bible makes it clear where the world, and each one of us in it, is heading. We will meet God one day and the plea of ignorance will be inadmissible and Paul tells us why: 'Since what may be known about God is plain to them [or rather, *in* them], because God has made it plain to them. For since the creation of the world God's invisible qualities—his eternal power and divine nature—have been clearly seen, being understood from what has been made, *so that men are without excuse*' (1:19–20).

If you were to go to any art gallery and view some of the paintings there, you wouldn't think for a moment that those works of art came into being all by themselves, would you? As you study the painting, part of your mind will ponder the artist himself, maybe thinking what an incredible imagination he has, what skill in transferring those thoughts via brush strokes and pigments onto canvas. Similarly, God has taken steps to make himself known through what he has made. God in himself is invisible and eternal, but through what can be seen in space and time, he communicates to us something of his divine nature, his divine artistry if you will. What is more, there is *within* each one of us a knowledge of God, perhaps more of a *sense* of God, an intuitive knowledge, what the philosopher Michael Polanyi calls 'tacit' knowledge—that awareness deep down that there is someone who has made us and for whom we were made, that we are creatures of a Creator (1:21). Sometimes this comes out by accident. It was the unbelieving Oxford philosopher, A. J. Ayer, who once exclaimed, 'Thank God I am an atheist.' Although we may not look around for someone to thank when things are going well, we can be sure we want someone to blame when things start to go wrong—then we look for a God upon whom we can vent our spleen!

But the problem is not that God hasn't spoken, the real problem is that we haven't listened. We have the truth, but what do we do with it? We 'suppress' it (literally, we hold it down)—push the knowledge below the level of consciousness in order to escape its disturbing claims (1:18). We may even say we *repress* it. Trying to ignore God is like trying to hold our breath, do it long enough and we blush with the attempt. So it is when we try to suppress this knowledge of God, do it long enough and eventually we blush with shame (1:21–4).

You do what you believe

Every belief eventually affects behaviour. No belief is neutral. Ignore God and there are consequences in every area of our life.

First, in our *thought life* our '*thinking* becomes darkened', says Paul. Instead of being wise, we become fools. Take the philosopher Bertrand Russell, one of the greatest atheist philosophers of the twentieth century. He was a genius. But he left his family destroyed, his followers disillusioned, as he lied and cheated his way through one affair after another. How foolish can you get?

Secondly, there is corruption in our *religious life*: They exchanged the glory of the immortal God for images made to look like mortal man and animals. Here we are at the beginning of the twenty-first century and has there ever been a century so steeped in superstition like ours? Intelligent people believing that the way you organise your furniture actually affects your well-being (Fen Shui); that crystals have powers of healing; or that the position of the stars determines our destiny. And Christians are often pilloried as being gullible! We are asked: 'What does it matter what you believe so long as it gets you through life?' That is the message of Steven Spielberg's film *AI*: fine if you believe in God and that helps, but it is no different to someone else believing in the blue fairy.

But there is a high price to pay in our *social life*, which is what Romans 1:24–32 is about. What spills out of our minds flows, into the bedrooms and eventually out onto the streets: 'Therefore, God gave them over in the sinful desires of their hearts to sexual impurity for the degrading of their bodies with one another. They exchanged the truth of God for a lie, and worshipped and served created things rather than the Creator' (1:24–5).

Three times Paul talks about God handing us over to the consequence of our moral error: 'God gave them over in their sinful desires' (1:24), 'God gave them over to shameful lusts' (1:26), 'he gave them over to a depraved mind' (1:28). In other words, the perversion *is* the punishment. We rebel against the Maker and go against the moral grain of the universe and we shall suffer for it, as surely as if we decide to defy the physical laws of gravity by jumping off a high-rise building, it just takes a little longer to work itself out.

Why does Paul take as his case example of the full course of social ruin: homosexual practice? When Paul talks about such relations as being 'unnatural', he is not necessarily saying that they are against the predisposed inclinations of those who are doing them. He is saying, that whatever the reason, such practices go against the natural order of things as *God* originally intended. He has Genesis 1 and 2 in mind here, that the Creator's intention is that sex, which is a good thing, is for heterosexual marriage. Therefore, to engage in homosexual sex, not only constitutes a wanton disregard for the Creator's purpose for which we are anatomically designed (the male sex organs to fit the female sex organs), but it also constitutes a defacing of God's image which is meant to be reflected in heterosexual marriage, the complementarity of male and female which together mirror the unity and diversity within the trinity itself.

We do not know exactly the cause of homosexual orientation. It would appear from studies, that like a lot of other sinful behaviour, it is formed by the affect of the sinful behaviour of others. Studies show that among male homosexuals, 67% come from families where the father is not around or is a wimp, and the mother is a terrifyingly dominating figure, and so the boy seeks tenderness in male companionship. Paradoxically, another 30% come from homes where the father is brutal and the mother treated like a door mat, and so the boy learns to despise women and identify with male strength. The remainder comes from neither background, but have been seduced into a homosexual lifestyle maybe while at school or by a relative. But the fact is *we all* express corruption in some way or another, and lots of influences may be at work, but that does not mean that such things become right. For a variety of reasons, we might be inclined to steal but that doesn't mean it becomes right morally. What is more, neither does it mean that homosexual practice is the unforgivable sin, as we shall see. But the further we move from God's design, the further we get out of touch with reality and end up hurting ourselves—and more and more medical evidence is now coming out on the harmful physical effects of homosexual sex.

By far the worst condemnation is reserved not for those who through weakness or ignorance find themselves drawn into this kind of activity. (And which one of us cannot find him or herself guilty of at least one of the things listed in Romans 1:29–31—insolent, arrogant, boastful, disobedient to parents? Remember for every one finger pointing at someone else, there are three fingers pointing back.) The greatest blame is apportioned to those who approve and promote such things: 'Although they know God's righteous decree that those who do such things deserve death, they not only continue to do these very things but also approve of those who practise them' (1:32). Let us ask: in God's sight, who will have to render the greatest account? The young man or woman drawn into a gay lifestyle out of loneliness, or the church leader I once heard extolling the virtues of a lesbian relationship he once came across because through lesbian sex, he said, the two women had discovered the 'love' of Christ?

Bad News/ Good News

Why does God allow things to get so bad? It is with a positive aim in mind: to cause us to stop, to ask what is going wrong and turn back to him. Just a moment's thought will soon reveal that our world is one which is well-suited for rebels like us, for it is a constant reminder that all is not well between us and God. It is a lost world, spiritually speaking. A well known Harley Street doctor, Martyn Lloyd-Jones, once first assistant to the doctor of the Royal family, said that it is bad practice to try and alleviate the symptoms of an ill patient straight away. Those symptoms—the spots, the aching joints, the high temperature—are often the best indicators we have of helping diagnose the real *underlying* problem, and of course that is what we want treated. So it is with God. Because of his love for our *eternal* well-being he sometimes allows the symptoms to run their course in order to make us realise that our world is a spiritually sick world and we need healing—desperately.

Where does that healing come from? From God himself. We can no more cure ourselves than a lame man can make himself walk. We need help and the wonderful thing is that God has provided that help. How? We were told at the beginning of this passage: 'I am not ashamed of the gospel, because it is the power of God for the salvation of everyone who believes: first for the Jew, then for the Gentile. For in the gospel a righteousness from God is revealed, a righteousness that is by faith from first to last, just as it is written: "The righteous will live by faith"' (1:16–17). What does that actually mean?

Remember, this is a church Paul is writing to, a group of people who are Christian *believers*. Here were folk who fitted into all the categories he has already described, those who had lived it up—sleeping around, who had swindled and lied and cheated their way through life, who had broken their parents' hearts by the way they had trampled over their feelings. In other words, they were people like you and me. What changed them? Paul says it was the gospel. The message that God has devised a way whereby people on the wrong side of him can be put on the right side of him, which is what that little phrase 'righteousness of God' means: being declared to be in a *right* relationship with God, with the result that however falteringly, they can start living God's way, by God's power. How does that happen? Through faith. Trusting that God, through his Son Jesus, the God who became man, has stepped into the breach and on a cross took the punishment and shame for our sin that we rightly deserve, so exhausting God's anger—paying the price. It is a message which also tells us he is now alive as the rightful ruler of the world and our lives, and by his Holy Spirit gives us what we need: not principles to live by, but power by which to live.

Changes lives

In case you think all this is abstract and doesn't apply to you, here are the words of a physics graduate called Rob: 'When I started as a student, you were likely to find me on the footie pitch or in a pub on a Sunday, certainly not in church. While I didn't have a religious upbringing, I did on occasions wonder what it was all about [exactly what Paul says about our sense of God]. Yet as a physicist, I naively assumed that only science held the key to the big questions of life. Coming to college was the first time I met committed Christians of my own age. To my surprise, they were clearly intelligent people who didn't seem particularly gullible. So I was intrigued and slightly incredulous that they could believe such fairy tales. Curiosity got the better of me and I began to investigate. One thing that struck me as I looked was the integrity of lifestyle displayed by the Christians. They had better, more real friendships and better attitudes towards other people [belief does affect behaviour!]. I spent a year asking questions and found consistently that Christians did not have *blind* faith but coherent and well thought out beliefs. Also, their honest analysis of human nature as flawed and self-centred and the radical solution being found in the cross of Jesus was compelling. As I looked I found that the real issue was about how *I* responded to a living person: Jesus Christ, not whether I believed in some abstract concept of God. Eventually I committed my life to following Jesus.'

Does that ring any bells with you? Do you feel lost in a lost world, wanting to satisfy that deep longing of your heart to know the God who is big enough and loving enough to take you back as you are in order to make you into the sort of person he wants you to be? Then why not start to make that journey back home to him? The route map is given in the Bible, Jesus Christ is both the guide and final destination. He simply invites you to take him at his word and follow him.

5

What's Wrong?
The Search for Forgiveness

Josef Vissarionovich was personally responsible for the deaths of over 40 million of his fellow countryman. He is better known by the name of Stalin which means 'steel', a name given by his contemporaries who fell under his steel-like will. Stalin once trained for ministry in the church and then made a positive and determined decision to break with his belief in God. Instead, he embraced Marxism and became Lenin's notorious successor. Always keen to drive a point home, once Stalin decided to use a visual aid to impress upon his comrades a valuable lesson in social engineering. Forcibly clutching a live chicken in one hand, he systematically started to pluck it with the other. As the chicken struggled in vain to escape, he continued the painful denuding process until the chicken was completely stripped. 'Now watch', Stalin said as he placed the chicken on the floor and walked away with some bread crumbs in his hand. Sure enough, the fear crazed chicken hobbled towards him and clung to his trousers. Then Stalin threw a handful of grain at the bird and the bird dutifully followed him around the room. He then turned to his henchmen and said, 'This is the way to rule people. If you inflict inordinate pain on them they will follow you for food for the rest of their lives.'

Stalin was an atheist. Or was he? According to his daughter Svetlana, as Stalin lay dying, plagued with terrifying hallucinations, he suddenly sat up halfway in bed, clenched his fist towards heaven, fell back on his pillow and died. So perhaps he was not so much an atheist as an 'anti-theist'—openly defying the God he knew to exist.

This may seem shocking, but the Bible's assessment of the human race is that given the power and the opportunity to live as if there is no God, then anyone of us could find ourselves doing what Stalin did. What is there to stop us, apart from lack of power and opportunity? Conscience? But what is that but the product of blind, meaningless chance and an evolutionary freak? Within each one of us there is this drive to be a god.

Why is the world in a mess? That was a question that produced a considerable amount of correspondence in the Times many years ago. The most penetrating and succinct answer was given by the Christian writer, G. K. Chesterton. 'What's wrong with the world?' the editor asked. The reply came, 'Dear Sir, I am. Yours sincerely, G. K. Chesterton.' What is at the heart of the problem of evil and suffering which plagues our world with its bomb blasts, its muggings, its drug abuse and behavioural breakdown in schools? It is, says the Bible, the human heart. Nowhere is this better illustrated than in Ezekiel 28 and the tragedy of the King of Tyre, which, as we shall see, is also your tragedy and mine.

Man's folly

Here we have man's folly (28:1–5):

> The word of the LORD came to me: 'Son of man, say to the ruler of Tyre, "This is what the Sovereign LORD says:
>
> "'In the pride of your heart
>   you say, 'I am a god;
> I sit on the throne of a god
>   in the heart of the seas.'
> But you are a man and not a god,
>   though you think you are as wise as a god.
> Are you wiser than Daniel?
>   Is no secret hidden from you?
> By your wisdom and understanding
>   you have gained wealth for yourself
> and amassed gold and silver
>   in your treasuries.
> By your great skill in trading
>   you have increased your wealth,
> and because of your wealth
>   your heart has grown proud.'"

What we have in this figure of the King of Tyre is the epitome of pagan man and woman. What is more, this model of pagan man has an enormous self-esteem problem, namely the problem of his enormous self-esteem; 'God says, "Your heart has grown proud."' The Bible sees the problem of a high self-esteem to be much more serious and far more dangerous than the problem of a low self-esteem. But where did the King of Tyre get his high self-esteem from? It flowed from his great achievements (28:4), in that it was by his wisdom and understanding he has amassed great wealth. The result is that his heart has grown proud (28:5). Here, then, is self-made man. Tyre was at this time a prosperous and highly influential city state: it is Washington, Bonn, or London. This King had political clout and he knew it. He was successful and secure.

When you think about it, this is the outlook that dominated most of the twentieth century and is still much with us in the twenty-first century. It is the maxim of the Greek philosopher, Protagoras, that, 'Man is the measure of all things.' It is the optimistic humanism of President Kennedy who said, 'Since most of the world's troubles have been caused by man [and on that score he was absolutely right] most of the problems can be solved by man.' On that point he was absolutely wrong, for that breezy optimism was sorely put to the test forty years ago when the world teetered on the edge of a nuclear conflagration with the Cuban Missile Crisis. Not that much has changed. The predominant outlook is still that with the right knowledge, the right resources, and the right will, crime on our streets will be reduced, terrorists will be hunted down and brought to account, poverty will be abolished and our environment will be safe. Both individually and globally we measure ourselves in terms of our achievements. We live for the future because we hope to achieve something in it. That is the case with the King of Tyre.

But you may say, 'What is wrong with that? We all want to achieve something: good exam results, a happy marriage, even a successful church.' Of course, in and of itself there is nothing wrong with achievement as such. But it rarely exists 'in and of itself' because such thinking is often accompanied by pride. It is the myth of *self*-achievement, *self*-sufficiency, *self*-aggrandisement that is the problem. For such thinking inevitably excludes God. Instead, we begin to believe too much in ourselves as *our* wants, *our* plans, *our* feelings begin to fill our horizon– individually and as a nation. In short, we begin to see ourselves as gods: independent and autonomous. We are often heard to say, 'It is *my* life, *I* will do with it what *I* want.' In some cases this is even encouraged, 'Believe in yourself, you can do whatever you want to do, be whatever you want to be.' Not so much the power of positive thinking, but the folly of wishful unthinking. When we have achieved things, especially by amassing wealth, and with it power and prestige, it does feed that delusion that *we* are in control for we think, 'If I have done this, what is to stop me achieving more in the future?' But what happens when people start thinking that they are gods, with a small 'g' as we see in v. 2? Pretty soon we start acting like 'gods' This doesn't mean that we go around saying 'I am god, I am god', like children in the school playground. But the behaviour we often display reveals that belief. The Christian writer, Professor Don Carson, gives a helpful illustration of this. He says, 'Remember when you have had an argument with someone and you have lost. What do you do? Well, you go home and you rerun the argument again in your mind. You think of all the things you should have said. All the things you could have said and would have said had you been quick enough to think of them. Now, in the rerun—who wins? I have lost many an argument but never a rerun. Why? Because I want to come out on top. I want to be god.' When a father in a family acts like this, we have abuse; when a group in a society act like this, we have race riots; when a country or a movement act like this, we have Belsen and 911.

It can all be traced back to the root of all sin which is pride, the word which forms the literary envelope of this section in Ezekiel 28:2–5. Why is this? Why doesn't God attack the King of Tyre for his greed or his cruelty? It is because it is pride which gives rise to all these other things and portrays most vividly the anti-God state of our minds. If you want to know how proud you are, then ask yourself: 'How much do I dislike being snubbed, put down, or patronised by others?' If the answer is 'quite a lot', then you have a serious self-esteem problem. The point is that each person's pride is in competition with everyone else's pride. Pride, by its very nature, is competitive. It must have someone else to look down on to thrive. Why is it that an incredibly rich person wants to get richer? After all you can only enjoy a finite number of cars, dresses, homes and so on. It is because in order to feel good, you have to be richer than someone else. And on it goes: 'I must beat that person in the exam, this person at sport, not because it is the aim of the game, but because it makes me feel better. There is someone down there I can measure myself against and then I can feel like a god.'

The writer C. S. Lewis puts it this way: 'Pride has been the chief cause of misery in every nation and every family since the world began. Other vices may sometimes bring people together, you may find good fellowship and friendliness amongst drunken people. But Pride always means enmity—it is enmity. And not only enmity between man and man, but enmity to God. In God you come up against something which in every respect is immeasurably superior to yourself. Unless you know God as that—you do not know God at all. As long as you are proud you cannot know God. A proud person is always looking down on things and people; and of course, as long as you are looking down, you cannot see something that is above you.' You may be reading this and are not yet a committed Christian—why? Is it that there is something in your life which you will not let go of because you want to be god over that particular thing: a relationship, an idea, a future career. Is the real reason pride, even intellectual pride?

God's verdict

What is God's verdict? It is that he, and not the King of Tyre, nor us, will be God (28:6–10):

> '"Therefore this is what the Sovereign LORD says:

>> '"Because you think you are wise,
>> as wise as a god,
>> I am going to bring foreigners against you,
>> the most ruthless of nations;
>> they will draw their swords
>> against your beauty and wisdom
>> and pierce your shining splendour.
>> They will bring you down to the pit,
>> and you will die a violent death
>> in the heart of the seas.
>> Will you then say, 'I am a god,'
>> in the presence of those who kill you?
>> You will be but a man, not a god,
>> in the hands of those who slay you.
>> You will die the death of the uncircumcised
>> at the hands of foreigners.

> I have spoken, declares the Sovereign LORD."'

We so easily deceive ourselves. At the turn of the twentieth century people believed that with science and technology at their disposal they were going to bring about paradise on earth. Blake's dream of building Jerusalem 'on England's green and pleasant land' was sung with gusto and conviction in our public and grammar schools. The result? Many of those boys were left dead, dying and maimed on the killing fields of Paschendale and the Somme. The science which was going to save mankind simply devised more efficient ways of destroying mankind. Of course, the 1914–18 war was going to be the war to end all wars, but within a short space of twenty years the world saw an even bloodier war and greater atrocities. This time, science was used to bring about a 'final solution' in the gas chambers of Auschwitz. This too was a time when God was pushed out of the picture and the conceit and hubris of man blossomed without restraint. But do you see what God was doing? He wasn't being inactive. He was allowing the overweening pride of man to follow its logical course—as he was doing here with the King of Tyre. 'You think that you can manage the world better without me, you are so wise, so proud and powerful, then go ahead, meet others who are also wise, proud and powerful and they will beat you.' Hitler said he was a god—although he didn't look too much like a god as his burnt body was dragged out of the Reichstag bunker in 1945. The stark truth is, none of us look much like gods when we shake our puny fists in defiance against the one who made us and loves us, when we think we can outsmart him and do a better job of running the world than he can. Yet, as we look around, isn't that precisely where we find ourselves as a society?

Man's tragedy

This brings us to the third section—man's tragedy. This is a lament contrasting what the King was, with what he has become. Here is Ezekiel 28:12–17, from the New Revised Standard Version:

> Son of man, take up a lament concerning the king of Tyre and say to him: "This is what the Sovereign LORD says:
>
> "'You were the model of perfection,
>   full of wisdom and perfect in beauty.
> You were in Eden,
>   the garden of God;
> every precious stone adorned you:
>   ruby, topaz and emerald,
> chrysolite, onyx and jasper,
>   sapphire, turquoise and beryl.
> Your settings and mountings were made of gold;
>   on the day you were created they were prepared.
> With an anointed cherub as guardian I placed you.
> You were on the holy mount of God;
>   you walked among the fiery stones.
> You were blameless in your ways
>   from the day you were created
>   till wickedness was found in you.
> Through your widespread trade
>   you were filled with violence,
>   and you sinned.
> So I drove you in disgrace from the mount of God,
>   and the guardian cherub drove you out
>   from among the fiery stones.
> Your heart became proud
>   on account of your beauty,
>   and you corrupted your wisdom
>   because of your splendor.

> So I threw you to the earth;
> I made a spectacle of you before kings.'"

Who is he talking about? He is speaking of the King of Tyre, as he has already said. So what is all this talk about 'Eden', being a 'model of perfection', 'blameless in all your ways', 'living on the mountain of God'? Using poetic language, God through Ezekiel is saying that we are never going to understand the tragedy of the King of Tyre, nor the tragedy of our lives, unless we realise what humankind was like when he originally made us. For this is *also* a description of Adam in the garden of Eden, and the King of Tyre, and indeed all of us, are children of Adam. This is when a man was truly King, the pinnacle of God's creation, made by God to live consciously in the presence of God. What is more, these are the heights from which we have fallen. The Bible views us as a little lower than the angels (Psalm 8); we now view ourselves as a little higher than the apes, and in some cases much lower than them because as far as we know apes do not rape, torture, and devise all sorts of evil in their hearts as we do (28:15–16). 'Wickedness' is found in us. We are filled with violence and we have sinned.

We no longer live in Eden, we are *East* of Eden, lost, wondering, homeless—far from living in the presence of God, we are busy hiding from God. The human tragedy is the greatest tragedy in the universe and heaven weeps for us.

If that is all that God had to say, the tragedy would be even greater for we would have no hope whatsoever. But he does have something else to say, through his Son, the Lord Jesus Christ and here we have God's remedy.

God's remedy

The King of Tyre is the exact opposite to the King of Kings. Jesus came to reverse the tragedy of the King of Tyre, which is the tragedy of humanity, by bearing our tragedy on a cross. This is the way the apostle Paul puts it in Philippians 2: 'He did not consider equality with God something to be grasped, but made himself nothing, taking the very nature of a servant, being made in human likeness. And being found in appearance as a man, he humbled himself and became obedient to death—even death on a cross. Therefore, *God* exalted him to the highest place.' God does the exalting, not us. Do you want to be restored into the presence of God? Do you want to regain some of the dignity and value you have lost? Then there is only one we can go to and that is the Lord Jesus Christ. He is no tyrant who will pluck us like live chickens, he is a loving King who is humble enough to take us as we are and slowly change us into the kind of people God wants us to be.

Why is the world in a mess? Because of us. Why is there hope for the world? Because of Jesus. Why don't you come to him?

6

Pure Evil
The search for goodness

In the summer of 2001, in full daylight in Birmingham, a 44 year old man, knifed a young girl as she lay out in the park sunbathing with a friend. A mother in South Carolina fastened her own two children snugly into their safety belts only to sink the car in the river in order to restore a romantic interest with a man who wanted her but not the kids. An upper-middle class college couple in New Jersey, Brian Peterson and Amy Grossberg, delivered a child in a motel room, then bashed its head and dumped it in a skip. Jeffrey Dahmer was a serial killer, submerging himself in cannibalism and necrophilia. The Milwaukee jury who tried him concluded that he was not insane, he was evil.

What does the face of evil look like? Maybe it is a red-eyed Hannibal Lecter peering at us from the shadows? Not really. It looks like the child in the playground, the old man next door, the girl on the checkout, the lecturer in the university; in other words, it looks like you and me.

The fact is we are in deep trouble. Not simply because such events which appal us are taking place with increasing frequency, such that in the USA from 1985–1991 the number of 16 year olds arrested for murder rose 158% and 12 year olds by 100%. Rather, we are in trouble in that we have a crisis in finding a category by which to explain such things. What used to be described as evil is now not simply being explained but is in danger of being explained *away*. Can we honestly say *evil* exists as a *moral* category anymore? Isn't it something else like 'sickness'? In other words, can we say evil exists?

Using a few broad brush strokes, let us look at the various ways open to us to try and understand 'pure' evil in the world, what are some of the 'road maps' of reality which are open to us.

Pure materialism

First of all, there is pure materialism. This is the view that everything is to be understood in terms of material cause and effect. The whole of existence is a result of impersonal, blind chance. This is the working assumption of most TV programmes. There is no great Mind behind the universe, there is no ultimate purpose either—only mere mechanism. Whatever sense we have of 'right and wrong' does not reflect any objective, universal, moral standards: at best they are an evolutionary device to ensure the survival of the species. Putting it crudely, a society which is well-ordered, where people care for each other, is more likely to produce the conditions conducive for survival—the passing on of our genetic material to the next generation—than one in which chaos and butchery reign.

Let us assume for a moment that this description of reality is accurate. Then what?

Then we are left living in a universe without morality. One person who saw with remarkable clarity and conveyed it through his writings was the Marquise de Sade. If nature is all there is, he argued, then whatever is, is right. There is no 'ought'—you cannot say you should or shouldn't do certain things because they are right or wrong. The moral category simply collapses into the factual category—the 'ought' becomes the 'is'. For de Sade the consequence was his cruelty from which he derived sexual pleasure. He wrote in *La Nouvelle Justine*: 'As nature has made us (the men) the strongest, we can do with her (the woman) whatever we please.' He did, hence our term 'sadism'.

If you were to reply that it is 'society' which defines 'right and wrong, what is acceptable and unacceptable behaviour', one can turn around and ask, 'Which society are we talking about? Nazi society? Headhunting society?' Society itself is but a product of blind meaningless chance and therefore its so-called judgments are ultimately meaningless too and are often the imposition of the will of those who have power. In fact, after de Sade, the one philosopher who saw that power is all there is left, if 'God is dead', i.e. he never existed, was Nietzsche who in the 1880s proclaimed himself the 'immoralist', 'the anti-Christ'. In his 'Will to Power' he said 'The world is the will to power—and nothing besides! And you yourselves are also this will to power–and nothing besides.' Might *is* right.

But this view, that there is no external morality and that nature is all there is, has taken some in another direction, which is hard to refute if we are going to be consistent. Ingrid Newkirk, the President of People for the Ethical Treatment of Animals compares meat eating to the Nazi holocaust. She says, 'Six million Jews died in concentration camps, but six billion chickens will die here in slaughterhouses.' Strictly speaking, if we are nothing but the products of blind meaningless chance, who can argue with that? We may be more complex than chickens, but who decides that complexity is of a higher value than non-complexity? Evolution? Hardly, that is an impersonal sifting mechanism and is incapable of making any moral pronouncements.

But there is a problem. For this view forces us to raise the question: Where does our moral sense actually come from? One person who has tried to answer this question from within a purely materialistic paradigm is Michael Ruse in his book, *Taking Darwin Seriously*. Here he says, 'The point about morality…is that it is an adaptation to get us to go beyond regular wishes, desires and fears, and to interact socially with people…. In a sense, therefore, morality is a collective illusion foisted upon us by our genes. Note, however, that the illusion lies not in the morality itself but in its objectivity.' He is saying that morality always carries a *feeling* of ought–that is where its power comes from. But there is no objective grounding for this 'ought' for there is no God or transcendent source of value. Our genes simply play a trick on us so as to ensure the survival of the species through what he calls 'reciprocal altruism' whereby the reproductive success of an individual is increased by helping others: for example,

I see someone drowning, I dive in to help them, and one day someone might do the same for me. Or it works by what Ruse calls 'kin selection'. We feel a stronger sense of moral obligation to those of the same blood because this will ensure the passing on of our family genes.

But if morality is simply to be understood as a self-preserving device that evolution has thrown up and therefore a trick to make us *think* that we are of value when we are not (after all a cold impersonal universe is valueless) then it *only* works if we do not recognise it is a trick, if we *believe* there is good and evil, right and wrong. But once we have seen through deception then we can discard it and say: 'If I get pleasure out of killing, I kill. Who cares about the survival of the species? We kill rats, dinosaurs haven't survived and the universe does not weep, why should I?' Indeed it works in the opposite direction and the evolutionary trick has over-reached itself, for now it makes sense to ignore its claims upon my conscience. If I realise someone is trying to con me, then it makes sense to ignore the con.

Some, however, like the champion of atheism Richard Dawkins openly admits that the way to answer the problem of evil is to deny its existence outright. So he writes: 'In a universe of blind physical forces and genetic replication, some people are going to get hurt, other people are going to get lucky, and you won't find any rhyme or reason in it, nor any justice. The universe we observe has precisely the properties we should expect if there is, at bottom, no design, no purpose, no evil and no other good. Nothing but blind, pitiless indifference. DNA neither knows nor cares. And we dance to its music.' In his thought, Dawkins is being consistent—

that is all you are left with if there is no God—no purpose, no value.

But can we live with that? Can you imagine telling a raped woman that the rapist merely danced to his DNA? Or tell the victims of Auschwitz that their tormentors merely danced to their DNA. Or explain to the loved ones of those cannibalised by Jeffrey Dahmer that he merely danced to his DNA. Any belief can be argued, even the belief of atheism, but not every belief can be lived.

Sometimes atheists use the existence of evil as an argument against belief in God. One scholar for whom this was a problem was the one time atheist C. S. Lewis. He wrote: 'My argument against God was that the universe seemed to be so cruel and unjust. But how have I got this idea of *just* and *unjust*? A man does not call a line crooked unless he has some idea of a straight line. What was I comparing this universe with when I called it unjust?... Of course, I could have given up my idea of justice by saying it was nothing but a private idea of my own. But if I did that, then my argument against God collapsed too—for the argument depended on saying the world was unjust, not simply that it did not happen to please my private fancies.' In other words, if believing in God causes you problems because of the existence of evil, not believing in God brings with it its own problems too. How do you explain the good and, by way of contrast, evil?

Pure Relativism
Which brings us to the next attempted explanation of 'evil'—pure relativism.

There is an important scene in the film *Pulp Fiction* in which the two main characters Vincent and Jules are on their way to commit a multiple murder contract. As they cruise through Los Angeles, laughing and carefree, they indulge in what appears to be small talk, discussing what hamburgers and quarter-pounders are called in France. 'Royale with Cheese' they joke. 'Is it because they go by the metric system that they have different names?' asks one of them. Now the point being made is a clever and serious one, namely that what we name things is relative to culture. *Words* are nothing more than cultural convention. An act or a thing has no intrinsic value. *We* decide what to call it—the metric system of one is irrelevant to the imperial system of the other. A quarter pounder with cheese is to one what a royale with cheese is to another. Killing the undefended to one is 'affirming the superior race to another.' Do you see how it works? Who decides 'what is evil'? One man's meat is another man's poison. It's all relative.

Another film which spells out the problem of relativism—what is right for you isn't necessarily right for me, so don't judge—is the film called *The Quarrel*. The main characters, Hersh and Chiam, grew up together but separated because of a dispute about God and evil. Then came the holocaust and each had thought the other had perished. Reunited by chance after the war, they become embroiled once again in their boyhood quarrel. Hersh, now a Rabbi, offers this challenge to his atheist friend Chiam. 'If there's nothing in the universe which is higher than human beings, then what's morality? Well, it's a matter of opinion. I like milk; you like meat. Hitler likes to kill people; I like to save them. Who's to say which is better? Do you begin to see the horror of this? If there is no master of the Universe, then who is to say that Hitler did anything wrong? If there is no God, then the people who murdered your wife and kids did nothing wrong.' That is correct. If there are no absolutes, then one morality cannot be said to be better or worse than any other—they are just different. *We* may prefer say, democratic morality, but then a fascist might prefer Nazi morality and unless there is something beyond them to which we can point and adjudicate between them, we cannot even say that Hitler was evil—he was just different, that's all.

Following the pure materialist or the pure relativist, why not abandon any meaningful talk of 'evil' altogether and just speak about sickness, a deviation from the norm? In other words that there isn't morality, only therapy.

Thomas Harris posed the question of genuine evil with brutal honesty in his book, *Silence of the Lambs*. In it, the imprisoned serial killer Hannibal Lecter, who cannibalizes his victims, is approached by a young FBI agent, Clarice Starling, who hopes to draw upon his insight to catch another serial killer who skins his victims called 'Buffalo Bill'. And part of the conversation goes like this: 'What possible reason could I have for cooperating with you?' asks Lecter. 'Curiosity,' says Officer Starling. 'About what?' 'About why you're here. About what happened to you.' 'Nothing happened to me, Officer Starling, *I* happened. You can't reduce me to a set of influences. You've given up on good and evil for behaviourism, Officer Starling...nothing is ever anybody's fault. Look at me, Officer Starling. Can you say I'm evil? Am I evil, Officer Starling?'

In 1973, US psychologist Karl Menninger wrote a book with the intriguing title, *Whatever Became of Sin?* The notion of evil, argued Menninger, has slid from being 'sin' defined theologically, to being 'crime' defined legally, to being 'sickness' defined only in psychological categories.

But if our bad behaviour is reduced to nothing but genetic and environmental forces—'It's not my fault judge, it's my glands'—then the idea of blame disappears altogether. I cannot be blamed for having a limp, so I cannot be blamed for being predisposed towards cannibalism—we are back to de Sade again who was a determinist: 'Nature has made me bigger than women, I like to inflict pain on women, I can and so I shall.' But what is sauce for the goose is also sauce for the gander, because the notion of 'praise' disappears too. If the evil things I do are due to forces beyond my control, then why not the good? To psychologise everything away (which is not the same as saying that there is no such thing as diminished responsibility—for example being compelled to do something by the use of drugs or hypnotism—but even diminished responsibility assumes *real* responsibility), is to make us less than human: mere biological machines. We cannot blame a machine for malfunctioning—neither can we blame humans. When we start thinking of ourselves as machines we will soon treat each other like machines. If a machine is broke and you can't fix it: get rid of it. So why not people? The door is then open for involuntary euthanasia.

Deep down, intuitively, we know that evil exists and we are responsible for our actions. We may think of it this way: If someone accidentally trips us up, and we fall down the stairs and we are hurt, we may not like it, and we may think the other person clumsy, but we do not feel anger towards him in the sense of *moral* indignation. But if someone intentionally *tries* to trip us up and fails, we do feel angry. Why? After all, we are not hurt? It is because we believe that people shouldn't behave like that, it's not fair or right, they *should* behave differently.

Therefore, if pure materialism on the one hand, and pure relativism on the other, doesn't explain evil, but explains it away, what does? Pure Christianity: the account we have of God and reality as we find it in the Bible which 'rings true'.

Pure Christianity

While the Bible teaches that evil is a reality to reckon with, a belief confirmed by experience, 'pure evil' as such does not exist. Let me explain why.

Evil cannot exist purely for its *own* sake. It is always parasitic on the good. Take cruelty as an example. Why are people cruel? Usually for two reasons: either because they are sadists, that is, there is a derived sexual pleasure from inflicting cruelty, or else because of something else they are going to get out of it, power, money, the fulfilment of an ideology, which is often power dressed up. However, there is nothing intrinsically wrong with pleasure, power, or money. In so far as they go, we might call them good things. The badness comes in by pursuing them in the wrong way, or too much. You can be good for the sake of goodness, even when it is of no benefit to yourself, for example, laying down your life to save someone else. But no one ever engaged in cruelty because it is wrong, it was in order to achieve something else—

pleasure, or power. Goodness is itself, badness is spoilt goodness. We might call sadism sexual perversion, but that presumes normal sex which can be perverted. Greed is the good appetite instinct gone wrong and so on. Now do you see why good and evil are not equal and opposite? The good is primary and superior, the bad is parasitic and derived, evil cannot exist without the good, but good can exist without the evil.

That is exactly what God's road map to reality—the Bible—claims.

The reason why we cannot shake off our feelings of justice, right and wrong, is because a good and just God originally made the world good: 'In the beginning, God created the heavens and the earth,' begins the Bible. He made creatures capable of making real moral choices which have consequences: 'God said, "Let us make man in our image, in our likeness, and let them rule."' You cannot blame a stone for being 'the wrong shape' as it lies on a hillside, but we do feel we can blame human beings for being in the wrong shape when they act in a way which is inconsistent with what can only be called 'natural law'. So we know mass murder and rape are *wrong*—not just sick. They contravene and offend against a standard which is beyond us. God has woven that 'law' into the fabric of the universe and embedded it into our own hearts attested to by our consciences, which accuse us when we do wrong. This is not an evolutionary freak, making us think we are significant when we are not, it is a mark of the Maker.

Our real problem isn't particularly behavioural or psychological, it is spiritual. Having reeled off a catalogue of depravity—envy, murder, deceit, malice—the apostle

Paul puts it like this in Romans 1: 'Although they know God's righteous decree that those who do such things deserve death, they not only continue to do these very things but also approve of those who practice them' (Rom. 1:32). In other words, our sense of right and wrong testifies to our dignity and our depravity. Unlike other animals we have a sense of morality, but we delight to go against it. My deepest problem isn't the 'evil out there', it is the evil within; what I am capable of doing if only I had the chance.

The Bible tells us that there is also a supernatural malevolent power at work in the world—a personal spiritual being who is not a second god, but who nonetheless has remarkable powers often working behind the scenes and through human agents who in surrendering to the Lie, promote wickedness. The Bible has a number of names for this being: Satan, the devil, the father of lies. In other words, we live in enemy occupied territory. This enemy of God loves the stench of death and destruction. (Jesus describes him in these terms: 'He was a murderer from the beginning, not holding to the truth, for there is no truth in him. When he lies, he speaks his native language, for he is a liar and the father of lies' (John 8:44).) This is not to be dismissed as the stuff of children. After the Second World War, two of the greatest sceptics of Christianity became Christians because they could not explain what happened on any other terms. The first was the atheist philosopher C. M. Joad, who had spent most of his life ridiculing Christianity, the other was writer W. H. Auden. It is patently obvious to any but the most dewy eyed romantic, that evil exists, that humans are not getting better with the passage of time, that we are fundamentally flawed and that dark forces are at work.

The Bible's story, however, contains not only the bad news of the problem, but the good news of the solution which is this: that the infinite, personal God, who made the world in which his creatures have voluntarily turned their backs on him and so have introduced the dis-ease (the wars, the deceit, the hatred and prejudice which acts as constant reminders that all is not well and that our relationship with God is out of sync), has taken steps to combat evil and rescue us from our mess. God is not indifferent to evil, he is implacably opposed to it. God's response to evil is not to ignore it and say, 'Oh well, it doesn't really matter.' Neither is it to deny it and say it doesn't exist. No, he faced it head on by becoming one of us, some 2000 years ago–as Jesus of Nazareth. Do you want to know what the face of pure goodness looks like? Then look at him. He spoke some of the most beautiful words ever uttered. Where there was sickness and suffering brought to him, he met it—healing the sick, raising the dead. Where there was evil, he confronted it, not just the demon possessed, but the evil and corruption ensconced in religion and politics. And it is there that perhaps we see the greatest evil of all, religion which speaks in the name of god, but which keeps people away from the true and living God. Politics which claims for itself the prerogative and allegiance belonging to God alone—so we have 6 million Jews killed under Hitler, 20 million Russians under Stalin. In his own day Jesus, challenged that. The outcast and fearful he took in and gave hope. He spoke of a time when there would be a new heaven and new earth—a kingdom—he called it, in which justice and peace would reign and death would be no more. A time when the prince of this world—the devil—would be cast out—and any who turn to him would receive the gift of *eternal life*.

Then came the darkest moment the universe had ever known: evil unleashed in all its fury and perversity, when people like you and me—good people in many ways—took their Maker and simply murdered him. Hammering his hands and feet to a tree, stringing him up like a lump of raw meat on a butcher's hook. As he lay dying, they taunted him, jeered at him. Had you and I been there, we would have done it too. But something else was taking place on that evil day. God was actually working his greatest good. In a way only known to God, the innocent one—Jesus—was suffering for all the crimes committed by a guilty humanity. The judgment we deserve he willingly received. That is why he cried out, 'Father forgive them.' The price has been paid, our moral debt is cleared. 'The Lord has laid on him the iniquity of us all,' says the prophet Isaiah. Proof of this came three days later when Jesus was raised from the dead, showing that the devil's trump card—death—had been defeated. Evil does not have the last say in this world—a good God does.

All those who turn from going their own way, and trust in Jesus Christ discover that they are set free from slavery to evil and have reasons to fight against it. Why else do you think that the schools, the hospitals, the freeing of slaves, the major factory reforms in this country were all promoted under the influence of Christians? God is against evil and so are his people. They are not perfect, they know that, that is why they need a Saviour. They also know they still have wicked inclinations, that is why they need a special power called the Holy Spirit. But they are on the side of the forces of liberation. Why not join them? This world is not the be all and end all. There is a transcendent invisible reality which God calls us to tap into by coming to his Son. There is a world to come, and a judgment with it, and God calls us to get ready for it.

The true God is not stuck on mount Olympus, secluded from evil, he came down from heaven and absorbed evil on a cross, so that we might know and taste his goodness. One New Testament writer puts it like this, speaking of the God-man Jesus: 'Since the children have flesh and blood, he too shared in their humanity so that by his death he might destroy him who holds the power over death—that is, the devil—and free those who all their lives were held in slavery by their fear of death' (Heb. 2:14–5).[1]

Do you want to know that freedom? Then follow the map.

[1] See Appendix for text of Hebrews 2.

7

The World Is not Enough: The Search for Life

Each film is seen by 500 million people in the first five years. The silhouetted, tuxedoed, pistol-holding figure is now as well-known an international logo as Coca-Cola. In Japan he is called Mr Kiss Kiss Bang Bang. He is suave, sophisticated, invariably surrounded by a bevy of beauties and never without a wry comment for every occasion, particularly having just dispensed another villainous megalomaniac to an early grave. While the new female 'M' may disdainfully dismiss him as a 'misogynist, dinosaur, a relic of the cold war', to the audience, he still affectionately remains James Bond, special agent 007. According to producers Barbara Broccoli and Michael G. Wilson, their aim is simple—to provide two hours of escapist, high class entertainment. And, by and large, they succeed.

But for the creator of James Bond, the writer Ian Fleming, Bond was much more than that. He was his alter ego. In many ways James Bond mirrored his own life, with the Bond family motto to the fore, 'The World is not Enough.' Educated at Eton and later Sandhurst, Fleming went on to pursue a globe trotting career as a foreign journalist. During the Second World War he served in Naval Intelligence and, like Bond, reached the rank of Commander. Also with Bond, he shared an obsession for high speed cars, women, gold, drink and good food.

What we see in the life of Fleming is the darker side of what happens when fantasy steps out into reality, when the world is not enough and style is everything. Take Fleming's view of the 'love' of women for example. He once expressed this to a friend as 'women are like pets, like dogs.' Fleming was never jealous of a woman's other attachments because, to be frank, women were not worth that much emotion. The same self-centred egotism showed itself in relation to his male friends. Lord Rothmere, the newspaper proprietor, extended his friendship to Fleming for fourteen years, not suspecting that all the time he was busily seducing his wife. When Lady Rothmere finally became pregnant, he divorced her, and much to everyone's surprise, Fleming married her. But Fleming was a sado-masochist, consequently she entered a life of frequent whippings and beatings, until he began to embark upon other adulterous relationships, partly because his wife's scars from two Cesarean births revolted him so much. On the screen, Bond may be charming, but when translated into real life, he is an arrogant, misogynist, soulless monster.

Finding meaning

When we buy in to the idea, as most of our contemporaries are doing today, that 'the world is not enough', that is to say, when we try to find all meaning and all value in this world *alone,* then nothing satisfies. Like Fleming, we invariably end up destroying and being destroyed. It was the philosopher Wittgenstein who said that, 'The meaning of the world is to be found outside the world.' The Bible made that claim many years earlier. Real purpose and lasting value are only found outside this world in the one who made it and some two thousand years ago came into it: Jesus the Son of God. It is to some of his words that we turn: 'Whoever wants to save his life (literally soul) will lose it, but whoever loses his life for me will find it. What good will it be for a man or woman if they gain the whole world, yet forfeit their soul? Or what can someone give in exchange for their soul?' (Matt. 16:25–6).[1]

When the Bible talks about our 'soul' 'psyche', it is not referring to some sort of invisible spiritual sunbeam inside of us. The soul is what you *are*, rather than what you *have*. You are made a physical, spiritual, psychological entity. That is the soul, the real you, if you like–the true self. Can you think of anything more valuable to you than that? How do you put a price on something like that? To lose your soul is tantamount to losing yourself. What, then, is the point in gaining all the money in the world if you are not there to enjoy it? Or, if in the process of gaining it, you are corrupted by it? You may still have quantity life, but next to nothing in terms of quality life.

---

[1] See Appendix for text of Matthew 16. All following numerical references in this chapter refer to Matthew.

What is the value in gaining fame and fortune in this life, if all of that is reversed in the next life, and the next life goes on for ever? That's what Jesus is getting at. Jesus is not engaging in polite small talk here. He is dealing with things we would often rather not think about, but which he wants us to think about because so much is at stake– our very souls.

The trade off

What happens when we think that, as far as life is concerned, 'The World is not Enough'? According to Jesus, three things.

First, whenever we try to find purpose, meaning in this life alone, we lose it. But when we stop, and turn to Jesus, we find it: 'Whoever wants to save his soul will lose it, but whoever loses his soul for me will find it.'

In the film, *City Slickers*, a movie about three middle class men undergoing a mid life crisis in which they decide to ride the range in order to find the 'cowboy within', the whole experience causes them to reflect deeply upon the meaning of life. At one point the lead character, played by Billy Crystal, turns to the others and asks, 'Do you want to know what the secret of life is?' 'It's this,' he says, raising his single index finger, 'It's One thing.' The trouble is that he doesn't go on to explain what that 'one thing' might be. But the Bible would agree that it is 'one thing', the one thing being God himself.

The problem we face is that we don't know where to look for that 'One thing' and we look in all the wrong places. We try to save our souls, as Jesus puts it, as if it were all up to us. We call the shots, make all the decisions, and decide what is valuable and what isn't. The result is that we lose it, such that lasting satisfaction never comes our way. But the moment we stop trying to please self and begin to follow this man from Nazareth—Jesus—losing our souls for *his sake*, then we find out what it's all about.

Some years ago the journalist Bernard Levin wrote these words: 'Countries like ours are full of people who have all the material comforts they desire, together with such non-material blessings as a happy family, and yet lead lives of quiet, and at times, noisy, desperation, understanding nothing but the fact that there is a hole inside them and that however much food and drink they pour into it, however many motor cars and television sets they stuff with it, however many well-balanced children and loyal friends they parade around the edges of it…it aches.' Isn't that true? In many ways, we as a country have never had so much, and yet we are a country littered with soulless individuals, ever seeking but never finding.

Mind the Gap

It is interesting that Levin speaks about having this 'hole' inside, because in the seventeenth century, the Christian philosopher Blaise Pascal said something similar. He argued that within each one of us there us a 'god-shaped gap'. That is, by nature, at the deepest level of our being, we were made for a personal relationship with our Maker–the One thing. But being as we are, we are not that keen on coming to him on his terms and so we try and fill that gap with all sorts of other things, but invariably fail, we 'ache'. That is because only one shape will fit the spiritual gap. When God ceases to be number one, nothing else ever takes his place. The paradox, says Jesus, is the more we have, the less satisfied we become.

Use it or lose it

Which brings us to our second point, namely, there is a price to pay. 'Whoever seeks to save his life', says Jesus '*will* lose it.' No question about it! We lose our true selves in two senses.

First of all, we lose ourselves by becoming less wholesome and unfulfilled people in the short term. Let me mention three modern day 'soul winners', alternatives to God, by which we try to save and satisfy ourselves.

There is, of course, materialism, trying to gain the whole world, or as much of it as you can manage. 'Make enough money and everything will follow' as one of the corporate lawyers said in Ally McBeal. And whether it is left, right, or any political shade in between, that seems to be the dominant outlook. But what does it do to the soul, what sort of people does it make us into? More caring, more contented? Hardly! A few years ago there was a documentary series on TV called *Hollywood Kids*. These were children of famous film stars and those working in the film industry. Materially, they lacked for nothing. You name it, then they had it. But in case after case after case, the one thing they lacked was love. They were poor rich kids; emotionally starved. Materialism never satisfies. It is not a material vacuum we have, it is a spiritual one. Sinead O' Connor has put the matter bluntly, 'As a race we feel empty. That is because our spirituality has been wiped out. As a result we fill that gap with alcohol, drugs, sex, or money.' She is absolutely right, that is exactly what we do. The result? We lose our souls.

Then there is careerism. There is an old French proverb, 'Work is worship.' And that sums up what most of us are doing far more than we are willing to admit. Even within many of our universities, the old idealism of pursuing knowledge for knowledge's sake, boldly going where no one has been before, has been replaced by a short term pragmatism: what will help me get employed? What will bring in the money? What will help Britain prosper? The result is that we live to work, not work to live. The late property developer John Redland worked hard all his life and made a lot of money. Upon his recent death, he stipulated that his ashes be made into egg-timers, and be presented to his bank manager and taxman. Why? Towards the end, reflecting upon the goals which had directed the best years of his life, he said, 'One day I suddenly thought I'd worked hard all my life only to hand over most of my cash to the bank and the taxman. When I kick the bucket, I may as well go on working for them.' Often, however, the committed workaholic deep down is on the run, maybe from himself, maybe from his family, but ultimately from God. It is a matter of 'keep busy and don't allow disturbing thoughts about the meaning of life to crowd in, for who knows I might have to change.' The result? You lose your soul.

But it has to be said that religion is one of the greatest soul destroyers around. As we shall see, with the exception of Christianity, all religions are attempts at DIY: Do It Yourself. Whether it is the supermarket approach of New Age where we pick and choose the essential ingredients which satisfy us, or the self-indulgence of ritual—formal or free, at the end of the day, it is us, rather than God who is at the centre. He, she or it, the idol of our own making, is there to serve us, to make us feel good, to get us out of scrapes. But our souls are destroyed all the same, for we become slaves to the thing we worship—a fabrication of our own imaginations.

The ultimate loss

There is a far more serious losing of the soul which Jesus has in mind. Not only do we lose ourselves now, and increasingly become less than fulfilled human beings, but we shall be lost in eternity. Jesus goes on to say: '*For* the Son of Man (another term for Jesus) is going to come in his Father's glory with his angels, and then he will reward each person according to his deeds.' He is talking about judgment day, and he—Jesus—is going to be the judge. Whatever we commit ourselves to now, as shown by our deeds—what we live for, determines what we shall reap then—the rewards. What is materialism, careerism, religionism, but a commitment to number one: self? We may want to wrap it up differently, but strip away the tinsel and that is what you are left with. If it is to serving self that we give ourselves in this life, then that is all we are going to be left with in the next life—no friends, no family, no God. Elsewhere, Jesus calls this hell. As we have seen, we may experience something of that in the here and now, that sense of lostness, loneliness, disquiet. But if we keep on, we shall experience it in all its frightening awfulness at death. Then, what will having the big house matter, or that string of qualifications after our name, or the number of women or men we have scored with in our sexual conquests? Jesus is serious. He teaches judgment and our consciences confirm that it is coming. You reap what you sow. If we say 'No' to God now, he will say 'No' to us then, giving us in death simply what we have wanted in life: life without God. That is hell, an eternal black hole in which we are encased in the cyst of our own selfishness. What is left of our soul becomes our prison.

What we need, and what Jesus brings here, is that eternal perspective. If we are honest, this is the problem we have with Christianity. It is not that the church is old-fashioned (so is breathing), nor that sermons are boring (as if our weekly outing to Tescos isn't),nor that science has disproved the Bible (it hasn't). Our real problem is that, deep down, our hearts are cold towards God and we prefer to save our own souls by pursuing the world.

What, then, are we to make of this question of Jesus: 'What can a man give in exchange for his soul?'

Real value

How much are you worth? What value would you place on your soul? What would you consider being so valuable that you would be willing to ask for that in return for your soul? Surely there is nothing—the world is not enough. There is nothing you can give which will measure up to your eternal worth. You cannot buy back your life from sin and the judgment that comes in its wake, and neither can I. But the good news is that God can.

When from all eternity, the true and living God looked at you, the creature he had so lovingly made, and saw how you set your heart on everything and anything but himself; when he saw the mess you and I have made, he knew that a price had to be paid for our souls to be set free and he knew the world was not enough. That is why he sent his Son Jesus into the world. Jesus tells us about it earlier on: 'From that time on Jesus began to explain to his disciples that he must go to Jerusalem and suffer many things at the hands of the elders, chief priests and teachers of the law, and that he must be killed and on the third day be raised to life' (16:21). There is a divine *must* about it all. This is what he is going to give in exchange for your soul: *his* soul, pure and sinless. There on that cross, covered in spittle, pierced with nails, naked and bleeding, Jesus pays the price for our rebellion against his Father. The cry 'My God, my God, why have you forsaken me?' is the cry of the soul abandoned to hell, bearing our punishment in our place, so that what we deserve he receives and what we don't deserve he freely gives—the cleansing of our souls and the gift of eternal life—when the God shaped gap is filled as the risen Lord Jesus comes into our hearts by His Spirit. That is what it is all about. That is how much you matter to God. God loves you so much that the world was not enough for you, a million worlds would never be enough to pay the price for your rebellion and mine: he had to give himself. And amazingly he did.

But you ask: how does it become real for me? We are told in verse 24, 'If anyone would come after me, he must deny himself and take up his cross and follow me.' There are three things you must do if you want to become an authentic Christian and know God personally.

First, Jesus talks about 'coming after me'. That is, you surrender to him as your Ruler and Rescuer. He is the only person who has the perfect God-shape, he is God. He is risen from the dead and rules this universe—all of it. You need to stop rebelling against him, recognise he has done everything to put you right with God and ask him to come into your life now.

Second, Jesus says 'deny yourself'. This logically follows. The reason we lose our souls is because it is self that is on the throne of our lives. So, if Jesus is to occupy that throne, we have to get self off it.

Thirdly, Jesus talks about 'taking up your cross and following him.' The cross in Jesus' day was an instrument of death. Anyone seen carrying one had only one future: public rejection and an early grave. We have already seen that to be a Christian, in one sense, means dying to self and living for Jesus, which is true life anyhow, so that is no great loss. But it also means being identified with him to such an extent that you are willing to be known as a Christian, that you are willing to risk being unpopular and thought of as being odd. Jesus leaves us with no choice. Follow him and you have eternal life, reject him and he will reject you, though he does not want to do so. But whatever, you cannot be a secret Christian, carrying a cross does not give you that option.

8

Spurned Love:
The Search for Mercy

There seems to be no limit to the lengths which people will go in order to be rulers of their own little world. Take the well-known atheist Aldous Huxley for example, the author of *Brave New World*. What was it that made this great intellectual an atheist? Was it that his razor sharp mind ruled out the possibility that there was a God? Was it that the arguments against God's existence stacked up more favourably than the arguments for? Not according to his own confession. This is what he wrote as to why he wanted the world to be one which was at bottom meaningless: 'For myself, no doubt, as for many of my contemporaries, the philosophy of meaninglessness was essentially liberation from a certain political and economic system and liberation from a certain system of morality. We objected to the morality because it interfered with our sexual freedom.' Certainly in my experience as a minister that is what I have often found. The reason many people claim they do not believe in God is because they don't want there to be a God to believe in. But this refusal to let God be God, and exercise his right to be the loving ruler of our lives, can have its religious forms as well. Here there is not so much an outright denial that God exists, but a remaking of the idea of god so that he becomes domesticated, the sort of god we would *like* there to be, namely, one who would indulge us without making any demands upon us. But the result is the same, our owner is cut out of our world—we want to manage our own 'vineyard' without any divine interference. What is more, just let him try to meddle in our affairs, and all the worse for him.

That, in effect, is the issue that Jesus is addressing in this parable.

Get the picture

Jesus' parable of the workers in the vineyard is not like the earlier parables of the kingdom such as the Sower.[1] Those were more obscure riddles which required a good deal of teasing out on the part of the listeners. This parable is more of an allegory. It is a much clearer story, where each item in the parable has a spiritual counterpart, a little like the *Narnia* series by C. S. Lewis. The earlier parables of Jesus had points which were more or less 'hidden', these later ones are more or less 'open.' Why? The reason is that Jesus is drawing to the end of his ministry. As time has gone by, he has steadily been unfolding to his followers both his identity and his mission. The turning point was in chapter 16 and Peter's

---

[1] See Appendix for text of Matthew 21. All following numerical references in this chapter refer to Matthew.

great confession that Jesus is, 'The Christ, the Son of the living God.' Jesus then goes on to explain that his purpose in coming into the world is to die as a sacrifice for sins and to rise again from the dead.

Now he is in Jerusalem, and opposition to him is mounting, as we see earlier on in this chapter (21:23), where the religious establishment round on him and demand, 'By what authority do you do these things?'—Jesus having just turfed out the money changers from the temple. This allegory is in part a response to that challenge. This is why he has 'authority'—he is the Son and heir; and this is what his own people will do—kill him. Those listening picked up the message loud and clear: 'When the chief priests and the Pharisees heard Jesus' parables, they knew he was talking about *them*' (21:45). Then what did they do? Feel guilty and change their ways? Not at all. They simply decided to do the very thing the parable warned they would do: 'They looked for a way to arrest him' (21:46). Tragically we have been doing the same ever since.

The person and teaching of Jesus have proved so uncomfortable and so demanding that somehow he must be silenced. Silence him by changing his teaching: cutting out bits from the Bible. Silence him by reducing him to one of a group of religious leaders from which we can take our pick. Silence him by, in effect, killing him again, destroying his reputation, mocking his morality, saying he was a man for his day, but not ours, since we have moved on. But as we shall see, these attempts at evasion are not only futile, but dangerous.

A message about the past

The first thing we notice in this parable is that we have a message about the past. Vines and vineyards were a familiar part of everyday Palestinian life. Here we have an account of one which has an absentee landlord, given over to tenants who were meant to hand over some of the produce as part of their annual rent. However, they have other plans. They want most, if not all, of the profits themselves and they are not subtle in making the point. When the rent collector arrives, they beat him up. And this goes on and on, until eventually the son of the owner comes along and they seize this as an opportunity to take control of ownership of the vineyard altogether. They take a calculated risk in murdering him, gambling on the owner being weak willed, or elderly, or too far away to take decisive action. After all, in Jewish law a person who could prove three years' undisputed possession of property could claim ownership of it and these tenants banked on that happening. It is a pretty miserable and vile story. The behaviour of these men makes the Mafia look like the Vienna boys choir in comparison!

In fact it is far worse than that, because the property of which Jesus speaks is God's property and those who have constantly tried to cheat him of it are God's people. It had been going on for at least 800 years. In Isaiah 5 we read: 'My loved one had a vineyard on a fertile hillside. He dug it and cleared it of stones and planted it with the choicest vines. He built a watchtower in it and cut a winepress as well. Then he looked for good grapes but it yielded bad fruit.' The wording is more or less identical to verse 33. Who is Isaiah talking about, and so Jesus too? He goes on to tell us: 'The vineyard *of the LORD*

Almighty is the house of Israel and the men of Judah are
the garden of his delight.' Now do you see how utterly
scandalous this is? This is Israel, God's own people, who
were meant to be his pride and joy, who should have
been producing spiritual fruit which in turn should have
made all the other nations sit up and take notice so that
they in turn would seek after God and find him. But
that is not what happened. They decided to rewrite the
laws. Certainly, many of the leaders kept up with religious
rigmarole, but lied and cheated their way through life,
took bribes and robbed people of justice, especially the
weak and vulnerable. And when God did send prophets–
his rent collectors– to plead with them and warn them
to change their ways, they beat them up. Isaiah, so
tradition has it, was sawn in two by a sword. The prophet
Jeremiah was imprisoned in a pit and on it went.

The tragedy is that it was the same in Jesus' day. John
the Baptist was beheaded, and the greatest of them all,
the Son, was simply hated.

But this is not simply a description of Israel. It is also
a description of our world and our nation and it may
well be a description of our lives. The Book of Genesis
tells us that when God created man and woman he placed
them in *a garden* he had specially prepared for them. He
gave them the privilege of being his co-workers to take
care of the garden and to enjoy all its benefits. But that
was not enough for them, they wanted to be the sole
owners, they wanted to be like God, not so much being
law breakers but law makers, *they* wanted to decide what
they wanted to do. The result is what is known as the
'fall', the downward spiritual and moral spiral which we
see in evidence all around us today. What does living

without God look like? It looks like Bosnia, Afghanistan, Zimbabwe, the Congo.

As a nation, Great Britain has been singularly blessed by God in the past, as these people had. For a thousand years Christianity had been the official faith of this land. We have been delivered from paganism in the distant past, from Islam in the Middle Ages, from a corrupt Roman Catholicism in the sixteenth century and from Fascist and Marxist dictatorships in the twentieth century. Christianity gave us our schools, our hospitals, our prison reforms and factory acts. Blessing upon blessing has come our way. But what have we done with them? Thanked the Giver? Hardly. We have taken them for granted, spurned his love, privatised religion and so our society steadily unravels with new laws now having to be introduced to control 8 year olds! How far we have fallen.

But you may wish to ask yourself: 'How kind has God been in my life?' Yet, still there are areas you will not let God into, there are secret sins you are busy nursing. The owner of your life might be allowed to have *some* fruit, but not all that is his by right. Is that what is happening?

If so, then look again at this story. Do you see how much God is showing his patience with his people, how much he loves them? He sends messenger after messenger, and in one last determined act he sent his son to them (in the original it reads *the* son—his one and only son) and says, 'They will respect my son.' That is how much God cares for a wayward world and wayward people. He is willing to send his one and only son. Could we want any greater evidence of God's love and care for us than that? Perhaps. So let's look at what happens to this son.

A message for the present

'But when the tenants saw the son, they said to each other, "This is the heir. Come, let's kill him and take his inheritance." So they took him and threw him out of the vineyard and killed him' (21:38–9).

What is it that convinces me of the untold potential for human beings to do evil—what theologians call 'original sin'? Is it what we would see if you were to go to Auschwitz today, the thousands of pounds of women's hair, the gas ovens, the pictures of abused children and clothing stacked to the ceiling? In part, yes. But what convinces me most of all about the wickedness which resides in the human heart, is that we murdered our Maker. That is what the cross, the killing of the Son outside the vineyard means. It is the ultimate insult, the supreme gesture of human contempt for the rule of God. It is the final snub which puts the lid on all the snubs that God has received from the human race.

At this point it would be all too easy to shelter behind the fact that Jesus' message was for his own present time— addressing first century Jews. 'Oh yes,' we say, 'it was all their fault. The Jews, the Romans, we all know how barbaric they were.'

Do you remember that old Negro spiritual? 'Were you there when they crucified my Lord?' Spiritually, we *were* there. Some of us were with the Roman bureaucrats—turning a blind eye to the injustice, as some of us turn a blind eye to the evidence for Jesus today. Some of us were amongst the smug religious leaders, impeccable in our orthodoxy, but wanting rid of a disturbing Messiah for the sake of a quiet life. But I guess most of us were with the crowd, maybe the same crowd that only a few days earlier had been shouting 'Hosanna', when all seemed to be going well, now shouting, 'Crucify, crucify'. Our hands were not the actual hands that drove the nails into his hands and the wood, but it was our sin which held him there nonetheless. In his mercy he cried out, 'Father forgive them for they do not know what they are doing.' But this parable shows us the remarkable grace of that prayer, for they *did* know what they were doing (21:45). If there was any ignorance it was a culpable ignorance. We living today have even less excuse than they had for we have the whole Bible in our hands, God's complete and clear revelation. We also have had two thousand years of the good that Christianity has done, so for us to walk away from Christ is to add our own personal nail to the cross.

A message regarding the future

Which is why Jesus gives a message regarding the future: 'Therefore, when the owner of the vineyard comes, what will he do to those tenants? "He will bring those wretches to a wretched end" *they replied,* "and he will rent the vineyard to other tenants, who will give him his share of the crop at harvest time"' (21:40–4). Who was it that answered Jesus' question about the action of the landowner? It was the chief priests and the Pharisees. They had actually brought condemnation upon themselves. Jesus didn't give the answer—they did, and so they are without excuse. They can spot a criminal act when they see one, but the tragedy is that they cannot see that it applies to themselves. Therefore, Jesus spells it out for them with three references from Old Testament scriptures, which Jesus takes as God's own authority (21:42).

First, a quote from Psalm 118: 'The stone the builders rejected has become a capstone; the Lord has done this and it is marvellous in our eyes.' In other words, on the building site the builders throw to one side a stone which they think is useless. Then they realise this is the cornerstone, the one stone which holds everything else in place, which God uses to build his new spiritual house—the new Israel, the church. Here Jesus may be engaging in word play because in the language Jesus spoke, which is called Aramaic, the word for 'son' is 'ben' and the word for stone is 'eben'—so the 'ben' which is thrown out and killed, is the 'eben' which is raised up by God to build a house. Here there is a hint that the death of the Son is not the end, but that the scriptures, including Psalm 118, point to a resurrection, so that those who trust the Son receive the blessings of the son: 'Therefore I tell you that the kingdom of God will be taken away from you and given to a people (or nation) who will produce its fruit' (21:43)—we are back to the parable again. Who are these people? Well, not the present Jewish religious establishment, that is for sure. Because they reject the Son, God will reject them. But their future is worse than that, hence the next quote which is a combination of a passage from the prophet Daniel (2:44ff) and Isaiah (8:14): 'He who falls on this stone will be broken to pieces, but he on whom it falls will be crushed.' In other words, for those who accept Jesus he becomes a cornerstone which restores them, but for those who reject him, that same stone becomes a rock which will crush them. It is the same person—Jesus, but he occupies two different roles depending upon our response to him. He is either our Saviour or our judge, and the judgement he makes is simply the judgement we know is right: 'He will bring those wretches to a wretched end' (21:41).

How do you stand in relation to Jesus, God's Son? Do you welcome him as the rightful ruler? Do you believe that God wants the best for you and that is what is written here in this book? Are you offering up the fruit of your lives to him, saying, 'Lord I want to do this for your glory'? Or like Aldous Huxley and these good religious folk in the story, are you keeping God at a distance, denying him access? Because one day he is going to demand access, and then it will be too late. There is no life better than the Christian life, there is no love greater than God's love and there is no greater privilege than being God's tenants.

9

TEOTWAWKI
The search for a future

In July 1994, twenty-one pieces of comet slammed into Jupiter, causing bruises on the surface almost as big as the earth. One scientist has concluded that every thousand years or so, our planet is visited by an asteroid with the diameter of a football field, travelling at 20,000 miles per second. It doesn't take the mind of a rocket scientist to imagine what effect such a heavenly invader would have if it were to land in one of our oceans. In fact, Hollywood has done the job for us with such films as *Deep Impact* and *Armageddon*. But we might shield ourselves from such pessimistic prognostications by contemplating the statistics involved (the likelihood of this happening in our own lifetime is rather remote), or perhaps by pinning our hopes that a real Bruce Willis might be out there to save the world from such wayward interplanetary debris!

But for others of us, it is not so much the fear of what lies out in deep space which is of concern, but what we ourselves are busy doing on earth. After all, we are the first generation to be raised under the spectre of nuclear war, the menace of universal famine is real as is the shadow of economic chaos—think of recent events in South East Asia for instance. Arthur C. Clark, the author of *2001 Space Odyssey*, said, 'No age has shown more interest in the future than ours, which is ironic, since it may not have one.'

Many, I suspect, would side with Arthur C. Clark in that statement, that we are co-conspirators in a cosmic suicide pact.

But such pessimism has not always held sway. Until recently, the dominating belief in the West was in the opposite direction, that we were moving onwards and upwards in one grand evolutionary design towards Utopia. But two world wars, Auschwitz and Hiroshima have changed all of that.

It was the philosopher Immanuel Kant who raised the fundamental question: 'What can I hope for?' That question is basic to us gaining any sense of meaning or purpose in life. What can *I* hope for? Especially in the light of such pessimism which is all around us.

What we think is true about life and existence in general will invariably affect how we live out our own lives in particular. If life, the universe and everything is nothing more than the product of blind, meaningless forces, coming from nowhere and heading nowhere— then where does that leave us? No one has put it better than Woody Allen in one of his more sombre reflective moods: '…alienation, loneliness and emptiness verging on madness, the fundamental thing behind all motivation and all activity is the constant struggle against annihilation and death. It is absolutely stupefying in its terror and it renders anyone's accomplishments meaningless. It's not only that he the individual dies, or that, man as a whole dies, but that you struggle to do a work of art that will last and then you realise that the universe itself is not going to exist after a period of time.' And then he says, 'Until those issues are resolved in each person— religiously, psychologically or existentially—the social and political issues will never be resolved, except in a slapdash way.' Either life is 'a tale told by an idiot, full of sound and fury' which is the logic of atheism and so hope is a word devoid of all meaning, or what the Bible teaches and millions of people throughout the world have been believing for nearly two millennia is true–that the universe is the work of a glorious, loving Author whose signature is written in the heavens he has made and the knowledge of whose existence reverberates deep in our hearts. This Divine Author, this Word, has declared that we matter and that the whole history is moving towards a dramatic climax.

Back to the Future
One passage in the Bible which spells that out for us is 2 Peter chapter 3.[1] It is all about TEOTWAWKI—'The End Of The World As We Know It.' In the spectrum of world faiths, the Bible gives a unique appreciation of the future; the passage of time is meaningful and directed, we are going somewhere. The Christian message isn't just about having Jesus in your heart while you live, nor even

[1] See Appendix for text of 2 Peter 3. All following numerical references in this chapter refer to 2 Peter.

just a message about going to heaven when you die. It is a message about a new heaven and a new earth which, in one shattering future event, will replace this old and corrupt world of ours.

As we have already seen in this book, there is a lot of pessimism about today, and with it cynicism. It was like that in apostle Peter's day too: 'In the last days (that is the period of time between Jesus' first coming and his second coming) scoffers will come scoffing and following their own evil desires. They will say "Where is this coming?"' (3:3). 'Things haven't changed much,' they argue, 'the world is the same old confused mess it's always been. We still have wars, earthquakes, crime—now spiralling out of control. Why doesn't God do something if he is going to do anything at all? Perhaps he can't? Perhaps he won't. Maybe he doesn't care?' You may well have sympathy with such sentiments. So some, even leaders within the church, have given up all belief that there will be a second coming—such outdated ideas are the stuff of cranks and sandwich board carriers they say, not sophisticated people who have embarked upon a new millennium.

Making life count for something

But why is such a belief hard to accept, that the One who made and owns this universe, who some 2000 years ago entered into the slipstream of history as a human being, the God-man Jesus, should one day come back to wind up the whole show and give dignity to our existence by calling us to give an account to him? Think of it like this: How would you feel, if as a student at the end of three years at university, having done all the hard work and the cramming, the university authorities were to turn around to you and say: 'Off you go, there are no exams, no degree either, but we hope you have had an enjoyable time'? You would be livid, wouldn't you? And rightly. You see, those exams, that assessment, actually give value to you and your work. So it is with God's judgement. If he doesn't judge us, then he is not much of a God and our lives amount to nothing, as Woody Allen said. But of course, there may well be those who do sweet next to nothing in their degree course, who do live the life of Riley and would be only too pleased to be let off their finals. So let us imagine that what they do is to set up a student society called the 'Agnostics Examinations Society'. They are a clever group. They debate and publish papers, arguing that the whole notion of finals is a bourgeois construct designed to repress undergraduates, a myth whereby fear is instilled so as to control the reading and thinking habits of students. They ask: 'Which first year has seen their 'finals'? None of them. Oh yes, they have met people who claim to have sat 'finals', but that shows how powerful and successful the myth has been— how gullible and brainwashed they have become. And when it comes to that book, called *University Regulations,* who can trust that? It was written so long ago and is so full of contradictions, after all, how can you have 'part ones' of your finals if you are not in your final year?' Do you see how it works? We can fool ourselves that all such talk of judgement day is like that. But what we are doing, says Peter, is being led astray by our own evil *desires*. It is not that belief in the second coming is intellectually indefensible, it is simply that it is morally uncomfortable and we would rather live as if the divine finals were not going to happen.

The witness of the Word

The first and most fundamental thing such sceptics ignore, says Peter, is the unanimous testimony of the Bible.

We have to acknowledge that many of us today are not as familiar with the teaching of the Bible as we should be. This has recently been borne out in some answers pupils have given to their RE exam questions. Here is a sample: 'David was a Hebrew King who fought with the Finklesteins. Solomon, one of his sons, had 300 wives and 700 porcupines. When Mary heard that she was the mother of Jesus, she sang the Magna Carta. When the three wise guys from the east arrived, they found Jesus in a manager. The people who followed the Lord were called the 12 decibels. The epistles were the wives of the apostles.' With such widespread misunderstanding about some basic Bible stories, it is not surprising there is a lot of misunderstanding about what the Bible teaches about Jesus' second coming!

Peter tells us that he is not saying anything new. From Genesis to Revelation, the Bible makes it absolutely plain that God's appointed ruler—Jesus—is going to return at a time we will not expect and set up his eternal reign of love. That is the thrust of verses 1–2: 'Dear friends, this is now my second letter to you. I have written both of them as reminders to stimulate you to wholesome thinking. I want you to recall the words spoken in the past by the holy prophets and the command given by our Lord and Saviour through your apostles.' Wherever you look in the Bible: whether the prophets in the Old Testament, or the apostles in the New, or the teaching of Jesus himself—the testimony remains the same, Jesus is coming, so we had better be ready to meet him. In the United States there are T-shirts which have printed on the front: 'Jesus is Coming, Look busy'. It should read, 'Jesus is coming, be ready'.

In the rest of the passage, Peter backs up his claim. In verse 5 he refers to Genesis 1 and creation, in verse 6, Genesis 6 and the flood; verse 7, innumerable OT prophecies; verse 8, he quotes psalm 90; and in verse 10, Luke's Gospel and a saying of Jesus—that his return will be like a thief in the night. In verse 13, he implicitly refers to Isaiah 65 with the mention of a new heaven and earth. You can't pick and choose with the Bible, taking out one bit about God loving us and saying I will have that and leaving the more unpalatable bits about God judging us to one side. It is a seamless robe, take out one and the rest unravels before your eyes. It is all or nothing.

There are three wonderful things the Bible tells us about this theme of the end of the world as we know it which should make us sit up and take notice.

God—His-story

First, the Bible tells us something about the relationship between God and history. In verses 5–6 Peter refers to Noah's flood. Whether it was a flood which literally covered all the planet or the then known world is still debated, but *that* a catastrophic flood did take place around the area of Mesopotamia is nigh irrefutable. The point is that God does act in history. He is not someone who set the whole show in motion and then retired: a cosmic clock maker. This God is passionately concerned about the world he has made and our place within it. He meets us daily with blessing, causing the sun to shine on the just and unjust alike, but he will also meet us in judicial discipline, as he did then.

If we are foolish enough to thumb our noses at our Creator and treat each other and his creation with disdain, do you think for a moment he will idly sit back and let it happen? Would you? Of course not, and neither will God. He will hand us over to the logical consequences of our practical atheism, as two world wars tragically show, and as the moral and social demise of our own society demonstrates all too clearly. Say 'goodbye' to God and you can say 'goodbye' to social stability.

History, as someone said, is just that, his-story. It is as much about God rolling up his sleeves and getting stuck into the affairs of human beings as it is us doing all we can to thwart his purposes. If God is working in history then it makes perfect sense that he will guide it to one grand conclusion with one final and climactic scene before the curtain comes down.

Will he come again? You can bet your life on it. What is more, all this is achieved by divine command, for it all concerns God's Word. 'But they [the sceptics] deliberately forget that long ago by God's word the heavens existed and the earth was formed out of water and by water. By these waters also the world of that time was deluged and destroyed. By the same word the present heavens and earth are reserved for fire, being kept for the day of judgment and destruction of ungodly men.' God creates by his Word, he judges by his Word, he saves by a Word— the word of the Gospel and God will keep his Word. He means what he says and says what he means, and so we had better listen.

A brief history of time

Secondly, Peter tells us about the Bible's view of God and time: 'With the Lord a day is like a thousand years, and a thousand years are like a day' (3:8). Think of it this way, time can only be measured in an arena where change can take place. Our bodies grow old, our cars wear out, rivers flow to the sea. But supposing we lived in a world which was changeless. What if our eyes could not only move left and right, but backwards and forwards in time, so we could perceive the horizons of history as well as the horizons of our globe? In short, what if we lived in eternity? What would our time look like from that perspective? Such a being would see everything within one moment, the end from the beginning. Nothing would take him by surprise, like the mind of an author conceiving a book, all the characters and their histories appear at once, their past, present and future, together in an eternal moment. Why should this not be the case with God and the world? He leaves nothing to chance. He is not thwarted by anything we might do so that he says, 'Oops I didn't see that one coming'. He is God, the Eternal One. So whether it is five seconds or five millennia, from the standpoint of his plans it's all the same to him.

Does 2,000 years seem a long time to you? It is but a mere blink in the eye of eternity as far as God is concerned. So don't be fooled into falsely thinking that because Jesus has not yet returned, he never will return. As Peter remarks in verse 10, the day will come like a thief in the night. The thief has made his plans, he knows which house he is going to turn over and at what time, and it would not be on for him to send a calling card beforehand. God is not going to send a calling card either, he expects us to be ready to meet him at any time.

Promises, promises

Which brings us to the third, and perhaps most important thing the Bible tells us, and that is about God's relationship with us: 'The Lord is not slow in keeping his promise, as some understand slowness. He is patient with you, not wanting anyone to perish, but everyone to come to repentance' (3:9).

Back in 1970, there were lots of Christians praying that the world would end and that Jesus would return. Personally, I am so glad that God didn't answer their prayers in the affirmative. Why? Because in 1970 I wasn't a Christian. I wasn't ready to meet with my Maker. Morally and spiritually, I was in trouble. Why hasn't Christ come back? For the simple reason that God wants you to be saved. He so loves you that he is willing, as it were, to put off the judgement so that you might come to him before it's too late.

Let's not make the mistake of thinking, 'Fine, I will put it off. I will live life up to the full, and when I get old, then I might give religion a go.' It doesn't work like that. If you set your heart against God now, there is no guarantee you will be able to open your heart to him later, quite the reverse in fact, it gets harder not easier. Judgement deferred is not judgement denied.

But what is the point of all this teaching about the Second coming? We are told in verse 11: 'Since everything will be destroyed in this way, what kind of people ought you to be? You ought to live holy and godly lives', and verse 14, 'So then, dear friends, since you are looking forward to this, make every effort to be found spotless, blameless and at peace with him', and again in verses 17–18, 'Therefore, dear friends, since you already know this, be on your guard so that you may not be carried away by the error of lawless men and fall from your secure position. But grow in the grace and knowledge of our Lord and Saviour Jesus Christ.'

Who do you think wrote these words: 'I do not think in the last 40 years I have lived one conscious hour that has not been influenced by our Lord's return'? It was Anthony Ashly Cooper, better known as Lord Shaftesbury. That man probably did more to improve the welfare of the poor and disadvantaged than any other single person in the nineteenth century. His view of the future affected his life in the present. He didn't want to waste his life, he knew one day he would appear before his Saviour and he wanted to hear those words which every Christian wants to hear, 'Well done, good and *faithful* servant.' He knew that what mattered, mattered, for he knew what was to be lasting and what was to be burned up.

That new car, those shares, even the university degrees, will not last, they belong to the old order and will be destroyed along with it. What will go on into the new world? What will shield us from the shame of judgement? Good lives designed to live in a good world resulting from a right relationship with God. We are not put right with God because we are good. We start to be good because we are put right with God.

How do we know that God passionately loves you and doesn't want you to perish, which is an absolute certainty otherwise? Because, some two thousand years ago, the God of history came into history as a baby. The God of eternity became contracted into a tiny speck of human stardust entering time itself, to grow, to change– to die. The God who is so passionately committed to us became one of us, going to a lonely cross, and taking upon himself the judgement which is rightly yours and mine. As Peter says in his first letter, 'Christ died for sins, once for all, the righteous for the unrighteous'. (1 Pet. 3:18). That's why he died, so that all the filth of our hearts, all the hatred and pride which is tearing this world apart, was in one moment in time poured upon the eternal One, absorbing to himself the divine anger upon it all. The judge was judged in your place and mine. He took the punishment which was ours. Then he was raised from the dead and now reigns in the glory of heaven, and is going to come back to claim the world and his people for his own.

The question is: Are you ready? Do you long for that meaning and direction in your life, getting put back in touch with the one who made you and who loves you and who is so patient with you? The good news is that you can. The way you do it is to come one-to-one in your heart to the risen Lord Jesus in prayer. To ask him to forgive you. To make you his child. Then follow the map to its end.

Appendix

Scripture Readings

Each chapter in this book is based on a scripture passage.
The full text of the passages for 1–4 and 6–9 are printed
below (NIV).

Chapter 1 - The Animal That Asks

Ecclesiates 1

1 The words of the Teacher, son of David, king in Jerusalem:

> 2 'Meaningless! Meaningless!'
>   says the Teacher.
> 'Utterly meaningless!
>   Everything is meaningless.'

> 3 What does man gain from all his labour
>   at which he toils under the sun?
> 4 Generations come and generations go,
>   but the earth remains for ever.
> 5 The sun rises and the sun sets,

and hurries back to where it rises.
6 The wind blows to the south
and turns to the north;
round and round it goes,
ever returning on its course.
7 All streams flow into the sea,
yet the sea is never full.
To the place the streams come from,
there they return again.
8 All things are wearisome,
more than one can say.
The eye never has enough of seeing,
nor the ear its fill of hearing.
9 What has been will be again,
what has been done will be done again;
there is nothing new under the sun.
10 Is there anything of which one can say,
'Look! This is something new'?
It was here already, long ago;
it was here before our time.
11 There is no remembrance of men of old,
and even those who are yet to come
will not be remembered
by those who follow.

12 I, the Teacher, was king over Israel in Jerusalem. 13 I devoted myself to study and to explore by wisdom all that is done under heaven. What a heavy burden God has laid on men! 14 I have seen all the things that are done under the sun; all of them are meaningless, a chasing after the wind.

Chapter 2 – Where Do I Come From?

Genesis 1

1 In the beginning God created the heavens and the earth. 2 Now the earth was formless and empty, darkness was over the surface of the deep, and the Spirit of God was hovering over the waters.

3 And God said, 'Let there be light,' and there was light. 4 God saw that the light was good, and he separated the light from the darkness. 5 God called the light 'day', and the darkness he called 'night'. And there was evening, and there was morning—the first day.

Chapter 3 – Who Am I?

Genesis 1

26 Then God said, 'Let us make man in our image, in our likeness, and let them rule over the fish of the sea and the birds of the air, over the livestock, over all the earth, and over all the creatures that move along the ground.'

> 27 So God created man
>   in his own image,
>   in the image of God
>   he created him;
>   male and female
>   he created them.

28 God blessed them and said to them, 'Be fruitful and increase in number; fill the earth and subdue it. Rule over the fish of the sea and the birds of the air and over every living creature that moves on the ground.' 29 Then God said, 'I give you every seed–bearing plant on the face of the whole earth and every tree that has fruit

with seed in it. They will be yours for food. 30 And to all the beasts of the earth and all the birds of the air and all the creatures that move on the ground—everything that has the breath of life in it—I give every green plant for food.' And it was so.

Chapter 4 – The Lost World

Romans 1

16 I am not ashamed of the gospel, because it is the power of God for the salvation of everyone who believes: first for the Jew, then for the Gentile. 17 For in the gospel a righteousness from God is revealed, a righteousness that is by faith from first to last, just as it is written: 'The righteous will live by faith.'

18 The wrath of God is being revealed from heaven against all the godlessness and wickedness of men who suppress the truth by their wickedness, 19 since what may be known about God is plain to them, because God has made it plain to them. 20 For since the creation of the world God's invisible qualities—his eternal power and divine nature—have been clearly seen, being understood from what has been made, so that men are without excuse.

21 For although they knew God, they neither glorified him as God nor gave thanks to him, but their thinking became futile and their foolish hearts were darkened. 22 Although they claimed to be wise, they became fools 23 and exchanged the glory of the immortal God for images made to look like mortal man and birds and animals and reptiles.

24 Therefore God gave them over in the sinful desires of their hearts to sexual impurity for the degrading of their bodies with one another. 25 They exchanged the truth of God for a lie, and worshipped and served created things rather than the Creator—who is forever praised. Amen.

26 Because of this, God gave them over to shameful lusts. Even their women exchanged natural relations for unnatural ones. 27 In the same way the men also abandoned natural relations

with women and were inflamed with lust for one another. Men committed indecent acts with other men, and received in themselves the due penalty for their perversion.

28 Furthermore, since they did not think it worthwhile to retain the knowledge of God, he gave them over to a depraved mind, to do what ought not to be done. 29 They have become filled with every kind of wickedness, evil, greed and depravity. They are full of envy, murder, strife, deceit and malice. They are gossips, 30 slanderers, God–haters, insolent, arrogant and boastful; they invent ways of doing evil; they disobey their parents; 31 they are senseless, faithless, heartless, ruthless. 32 Although they know God's righteous decree that those who do such things deserve death, they not only continue to do these very things but also approve of those who practice them.

Chapter 6 – Pure Evil

Hebrews 2

14 Since the children have flesh and blood, he too shared in their humanity so that by his death he might destroy him who holds the power of death—that is, the devil— 15 and free those who all their lives were held in slavery by their fear of death. 16 For surely it is not angels he helps, but Abraham's descendants. 17 For this reason he had to be made like his brothers in every way, in order that he might become a merciful and faithful high priest in service to God, and that he might make atonement for the sins of the people. 18 Because he himself suffered when he was tempted, he is able to help those who are being tempted.

Chapter 7 – The World is not Enough

Matthew 16

24 Then Jesus said to his disciples, "If anyone would come after me, he must deny himself and take up his cross and follow me. 25 For whoever wants to save his life will lose it, but whoever loses his life for me will find it. 26 What good will it be for a man if he gains the whole world, yet forfeits his soul? Or what can a man give in exchange for his soul? 27 For the Son of Man is going to come in his Father's glory with his angels, and then he will reward each person according to what he has done."

Chapter 8 – Spurned Love

Matthew 21

33 "Listen to another parable: There was a landowner who planted a vineyard. He put a wall around it, dug a winepress in it and built a watchtower. Then he rented the vineyard to some farmers and went away on a journey. 34 When the harvest time approached, he sent his servants to the tenants to collect his fruit.

35 "The tenants seized his servants; they beat one, killed another, and stoned a third. 36 Then he sent other servants to them, more than the first time, and the tenants treated them the same way. 37 Last of all, he sent his son to them. 'They will respect my son,' he said.

38 "But when the tenants saw the son, they said to each other, 'This is the heir. Come, let's kill him and take his inheritance.' 39 So they took him and threw him out of the vineyard and killed him.

40 "Therefore, when the owner of the vineyard comes, what will he do to those tenants?"

41 "He will bring those wretches to a wretched end," they replied, "and he will rent the vineyard to other tenants, who will

give him his share of the crop at harvest time." 42 Jesus said to them, "Have you never read in the Scriptures:

"'The stone the builders rejected
has become the capstone;
the Lord has done this,
and it is marvellous in our eyes'?

43 "Therefore I tell you that the kingdom of God will be taken away from you and given to a people who will produce its fruit. 44 He who falls on this stone will be broken to pieces, but he on whom it falls will be crushed."

45 When the chief priests and the Pharisees heard Jesus' parables, they knew he was talking about them. 46 They looked for a way to arrest him, but they were afraid of the crowd because the people held that he was a prophet.

Chapter 9 – TEOTWAWKI

2 Peter 3

1 Dear friends, this is now my second letter to you. I have written both of them as reminders to stimulate you to wholesome thinking. 2 I want you to recall the words spoken in the past by the holy prophets and the command given by our Lord and Saviour through your apostles.

3 First of all, you must understand that in the last days scoffers will come, scoffing and following their own evil desires. 4 They will say, "Where is this 'coming' he promised? Ever since our fathers died, everything goes on as it has since the beginning of creation." 5 But they deliberately forget that long ago by God's word the heavens existed and the earth was formed out of water and by water. 6 By these waters also the world of that time was deluged and destroyed. 7 By the same word the present heavens and earth

are reserved for fire, being kept for the day of judgment and destruction of ungodly men.

8 But do not forget this one thing, dear friends: With the Lord a day is like a thousand years, and a thousand years are like a day. 9 The Lord is not slow in keeping his promise, as some understand slowness. He is patient with you, not wanting anyone to perish, but everyone to come to repentance.

10 But the day of the Lord will come like a thief. The heavens will disappear with a roar; the elements will be destroyed by fire, and the earth and everything in it will be laid bare.

11 Since everything will be destroyed in this way, what kind of people ought you to be? You ought to live holy and godly lives 12 as you look forward to the day of God and speed its coming. That day will bring about the destruction of the heavens by fire, and the elements will melt in the heat. 13 But in keeping with his promise we are looking forward to a new heaven and a new earth, the home of righteousness.

Bibliography and Further Reading

How Now Shall we Live? Charles Colson, (Marshall Pickering, 1999).

Long Journey Home. Os Guiness, (Water Brook, 2001).

The Call. Os Guiness, (Spring Harvest, 2001).

Can Man Live without God? Ravi Zacharias, (Word Publishing Group, 1994).

Deliver Us from Evil. Ravi Zacharias, (Word Publishing, 1996).

Christian Focus Publications
publishes books for all ages

Our mission statement –

STAYING FAITHFUL
In dependence upon God we seek to help make His infallible Word, the Bible, relevant. Our aim is to ensure that the Lord Jesus Christ is presented as the only hope to obtain forgiveness of sin, live a useful life and look forward to heaven with Him.

REACHING OUT
Christ's last command requires us to reach out to our world with His gospel. We seek to help fulfill that by publishing books that point people towards Jesus and help them develop a Christ-like maturity. We aim to equip all levels of readers for life, work, ministry and mission.

Books in our adult range are published in three imprints.

Christian Focus contains popular works including biographies, commentaries, basic doctrine and Christian living. Our children's books are also published in this imprint.

Mentor focuses on books written at a level suitable for Bible College and seminary students, pastors, and other serious readers. The imprint includes commentaries, doctrinal studies, examination of current issues and church history.

Christian Heritage contains classic writings from the past.

Christian Focus Publications, Ltd
Geanies House, Fearn,
Ross-shire, IV20 1TW, Scotland
info@christianfocus.com